HUSBAND
AFTER
GOD

Drawing Closer To God & Your Wife

Aaron & Jennifer Smith

A HUSBAND REVOLUTION RESOURCE

HUSBAND AFTER GOD
DRAWING CLOSER TO GOD AND YOUR WIFE

Copyright © 2015 Smith Family Resources, Inc

Publisher: Smith Family Resources, Inc
Authors: Aaron Smith & Jennifer Smith
Formatted By: Aaron Smith
Cover Art By: Aaron Smith

All rights reserved. No part of this book may be reproduced
in any form by any electronic or mechanical means including
photocopying, recording, or information storage and retrieval
without permission in writing from the author.

ISBN-13: 978-0-9863667-0-3
ISBN-10: 0986366706
LCCN: 2015910636

HusbandRevolution.com
Facebook.com/husbandrevolution
Twitter.com/husbandrevo
Instagram.com/Husbandrevolution

Give feedback on the book at:
HusbandAfterGod.com

Printed in U.S.A

Disclaimer: *The content in this devotional although rooted in
Biblical principles are the expressed interpretations and opinions
of Aaron & Jennifer Smith. We are not licensed professionals. There
are certain situations in a marriage that may need the assistance of
professionals or authorities, such as abuse. Please do not hesitate
to seek professional help.*

DEDICATION

Thank You Lord, for Your patience and
love for me and my wife. You deserve
all the glory and honor forever. In Your
precious Son's name, amen!

CONTENTS

Dedication   3
Introduction   7
A Special Note From Husband Revolution   13

Day 01: God's Purpose For Your Marriage   15
Day 02: Marriage By Design   21
Day 03: Lead By Example   27
Day 04: Your Wife Is a Gift   33
Day 05: Sacrificial Love   39
Day 06: Be Reconciled   45
Day 07: Set Yourself Apart   51
Day 08: Be Brave   57
Day 09: Protecting Your Marriage   63
Day 10: The Good Fight   71
Day 11: God's Economy   77
Day 12: The Armor Of God   83
Day 13: Pride   91
Day 14: Forgiveness   97
Day 15: Anger   103
Day 16: Love Her   109
Day 17: Wisdom   115
Day 18: Words Matter   121
Day 19: Called Out   127
Day 20: Prayer For You   133
Day 21: Prayer For Your Wife   139
Day 22: Prayer For Your Marriage   145
Day 23: Unity In Christ   151
Day 24: The Parts Of Marriage   157
Day 25: God's Order   163
Day 26: Avoiding God   169
Day 27: Abiding In God   175
Day 28: Intimacy In Marriage   181
Day 29: Walk In Victory   187
Day 30: The Husband Revolution   193

31 Prayers For My Wife Book   199

INTRODUCTION

You are here because God pursued you. You are a man who God finds incredibly valuable. God has set aside a very special opportunity for husbands and wives to experience an intimate relationship with each other, which reflects the intimacy God desires to have with all of humanity! Your role as a husband is extraordinary in that you have been required to love and care for your wife just as Christ loves the church. Loving your wife to this degree is not an option.

Unfortunately, you live in a fallen world--your culture, environment, and family tree have influenced who you are today, and not all of the things you have learned along the way are beneficial. You can probably think about a few things right now that you know you need to work on. The more you humble yourself before God and ask Him to transform you, the better you become at fulfilling your purpose as a husband, which in turn leads to the fulfillment of a healthy, joyful, God-centered marriage. Of course, reaching the goal of a healthy, joyful, God-centered marriage will also require your wife to take action if she has not done so already. Your wife may be ahead of you in this area, she may be right alongside you, she may be ten steps behind you, or perhaps on a different path altogether. Wherever your wife is spiritually, you need to trust God with her heart and continue to pray for her no matter what. Your wife needs you to do the same things you would want from her: to cheer her on, to set an example, to have faith, and to pursue her passionately.

As a Christian and as a husband there is a responsibility to nurture both your relationship with God and your wife. Failure to passionately pursue these relationships will result in isolation. You may know that feeling all too well, but you can stand again and fight for what God has gifted to you. To do so you must take hold of your responsibilities and commit to working towards growth and oneness.

This devotional is designed to walk you through an intense journey of experiencing God, specifically tailored to your first and most important ministry role-- being a husband! Here are some scriptures that support the purpose of this devotional:

PLEASE READ:
James 4:8, Hebrews 10:22, Colossians 2:2-3

These scriptures are foundational to the purpose of this devotional. God has called you to draw close to Him, to know the message of Christ, and to be encouraged. These things occur when you meditate on His Word.

This devotional has 30 chapters. So, for the next 30 days you are committing to the following:

- **Spending quality time with God daily by reading God's Word, praying, and journaling.**
- **Actively engaging and participating in all of the given challenges within each chapter.**

You may or may not be familiar with spending time with God on a daily basis. Whether you are experienced with this or not, here are a few quick tips on how you can spend quality time with God:

YOU WILL NEED A BIBLE.

It is written in Hebrews 4:12 that God's Word is living and active, so just as you would carry a conversation with a close friend, God will converse with you through His Word. Feel free to explore different versions and translations as you are going through scriptures. Reflecting on different translations can provide more understanding.

YOU WILL BE ENCOURAGED TO JOURNAL.

Writing is one of the most comprehensive ways to learn because it forces you to slow down in your thinking process, allowing your hand a chance to translate your thought. It is also very beneficial in that you will have the opportunity to refer back to any archived entry and see your relationship growth with God along with any answered or unanswered prayers you may have written down. This journal has space for you to journal within each chapter, but you may also use your own journal if you wish.

Here is a journal entry excerpt for you to use as a guideline; however, there is freedom to customize your personal journal:

EXAMPLE JOURNAL ENTRY

(Date) 11-24-10

(What God Is Teaching You) I need to stop worrying and give all of my cares to God. I need to keep praying every day. I need to lean on God's understanding and not my own.

(Answer Questions From Devotional) My worry stems from fears or insecurities that I won't have enough to get by.

(Prayer) God, please help me not to worry about my kids or my job. Please give me confidence in the plans you have for me. I pray that you bless my wife and give her patience today. May your will be done in my life. Amen!

When you spend quality time with God, growth in your relationship with Him is inevitable. The amount of time you spend with God and the length of your journal entry is completely up to you, just be sure to pray, read scripture, and record what you experience as you journal. Remember, God wants to hear from you, and He wants you to listen, the balance of both of these will result in great communication--the key to any thriving relationship.

Consistency is very crucial, both in your quality time with God and in participating in the challenges. Consistency reflects commitment and self-discipline. Some of the challenges will be more difficult than others; however, the result is a stronger relationship with God and with your wife. You must understand that this devotional is only as effective as you are willing to commit, and the devotion you exert, especially in your relationship with God, will overflow into your relationship with your wife.

Additionally, each chapter has a Status Update Challenge. This is an incredible way for you to share your journey through the Devotional with the Husband Revolution Community and get other husbands excited about participating. All you need to do is copy the status update and send it out through your preferred social media platform, being sure to tag @husbandrevolution and #HusbandAfterGod.

By committing to these standards, you will allow God to transform your life, your marriage, and countless others who you will positively affect through living as an example of a Husband After God!

Dear Lord,

Thank You for the husband reading this right now. God, I pray that You would begin to prepare this man's heart for the journey You are going to take him on. Use this devotional to draw him close to Your heart God, and use it to teach him how to love his wife better.

In Jesus' name, AMEN!

A SPECIAL NOTE FROM THE AUTHOR

I am excited for you to go through this resource and I urge you to invite a few other husbands to grab a devotional and go through it at the same time. You could plan to meet at a local coffee shop or grab an early bird breakfast and have some great discussion together over the material; you can keep each other accountable to the commitment you made, and learn how it is impacting each other's marriage! I have found that community is vital. Spur one another on toward righteousness.

Aaron Smith

GOD'S PURPOSE FOR YOUR MARRIAGE

Genesis 1:26, Genesis 2:7, Mark 10:6-9, Ephesians 5:25-33

God, the Creator of the universe, made man in His image. He made you in His likeness. As He formed you, He gave you life, breathing His air into your lungs. Unlike what the world would like you to believe, your existence is no random event.

You were crafted with intentionality and born with a purpose. God designed you in His image; this means you are a reflection of Him. You are living proof that God is real. Do not take this understanding lightly, do not just push it aside. Allow this truth to sink into your mind and heart. Take a moment to contemplate the fact that you were created for the purpose of reflecting the Creator and for the purpose of glorifying Him.

From the beginning of creation, God intentionally established man with authority to rule. With that authority comes great responsibility. Exercising authority and fulfilling responsibility require intelligence, yet another mark of God's incredible design, which distinguishes mankind from all of creation. You are intelligent. You can comprehend, discern, contemplate, question, reason and invent. Your mind, your intellect, is a powerful gift that God has given to you so that you may be more like Him.

In the same way that God created you with a purpose to reflect Him, He also created marriage with a very specific purpose. God gave us the covenant of marriage as an awesome symbol of the relationship He desires to have with mankind. He has given you an opportunity, unlike any other, to experience deep love, the kind of love that Jesus has for the church. The union between you and your wife is purposed to reflect the Gospel so that the world may come to know Jesus.

Just as Jesus demonstrated selfless, sacrificial love, you can imitate that same love toward your wife, and she can do the same for you. Marriage is an opportunity to bring glory to God as you share with the world His testimony by loving your wife the way Christ loves the Church. God's purpose for your marriage is to allow you and your wife to be a living representation of Christ's love.

As you grasp the weight of this purpose, it should begin to invoke in you a very significant question that you should be able to answer.

"Does my marriage reflect the Gospel?"

Dear Lord,

Thank You for creating me with purpose and intentionality. Thank You for trusting me with Your image and likeness. Teach me how to reflect Your character more in my life and my marriage. Help me to love my wife the way You love the church. Please shape my character to produce fruitfulness and every good thing. Show me how to live out Your purpose for my life. Please help me to be confident in my purpose, never doubting, never being tossed back and forth. I pray that my marriage is a blessing to my wife and others. I pray my marriage reflects Your love and testimony, Your ministry of reconciliation.

In Jesus' name, AMEN!

Share & discuss with your wife what you are learning about the purpose of marriage.

STATUS UPDATE: @husbandrevolution I will strive to reflect the image and character of God in my marriage! #HusbandAfterGod

JOURNAL QUESTIONS:
Why is it important to know God's purpose for your marriage?

What are a few characteristics of God?

How does knowing your marriage has a significant purpose change the way you look at your life/marriage?

What is one thing you will do differently in your marriage knowing that you are reflecting God's love for the world?

MARRIAGE BY DESIGN

Romans 1:20, Ephesians 5:21-33, 1 John 4:19,
Colossians 3:13

In the beginning, God created the Earth as we know it. He created day and night, He created dry land, named the seas and made all plant life, He created the sun, moon and stars, He created living creatures...then God created man. Everything that He created was for you so that you would know without a doubt that He is who He says He is. He also created it so that you would gain a greater understanding of who He is.

God did this so that no one would have an excuse not to know Him.

When you look at the sky and the stars, you see God's infinite size. When you look at the mountains and the trees, you see God's perfect patience and incredible strength. When you look at the vastness of seas, you get a glimpse at His unsearchable depths and the overwhelming weight of His glory. When you see the birds flying through the sky, you see His gracefulness and provision. When you see your breath on a cold night, you are seeing the very breath God breathed into your lungs when He gave you life.

Just like the rest of creation, God designed marriage with a similar purpose, to teach us about Him and His love for us

God clearly outlines His design for marriage in His Word, commanding that wives are to respect and submit to their own husbands, and husbands are to love their wives as Christ loves the church.

You are to love your wife with an unconditional Christ-like love and your motivation to unconditionally love your wife must come directly from an intimate relationship with God. Only God can give you the strength necessary to love her in this way. You love because He first loved you. You forgive because He has forgiven you. Your love is motivated by His.

There may be moments that your wife will do something or say something that stirs frustration in your heart. She may disrespect you, be unsubmissive or she may reject your invitation for intimacy. Loving her unconditionally, means that you fulfill this part of God's design for you as a husband, regardless of your wife choosing to do these things. You will always be responsible for the choices you make. Choose to be honorable, righteous and loving without conditions.

Your obedience to God should never be contingent on your wife's actions. You are responsible for your portion of the covenant you entered into.

By now you may be seeing this profound picture forming of God's design and purpose for marriage, for your marriage. Your marriage is not simply a relationship between you and your wife, rather it is intended to be a divine picture of God's redemption plan for mankind.

You have been given a gift of learning what it means to be like Christ in the most literal way possible, by loving your wife. With this new understanding of the design of marriage, you no longer have any excuse for not knowing God or understanding His plan for your life. Your new goal should be to daily pursue a marriage that looks more and more like Christ and the church.

Dear Lord,

Thank You for showing me who You are through Your creation. I pray that I can be more aware of nature and all that You have made. Open my eyes to the wonder of Your design. Give me a passion to comprehend the science of Your design. I pray I never make excuses for why I don't spend time with You. Help me to make it a priority to have quality time with You daily. Thank You for allowing me the opportunity to learn to be like You in how I love my wife. Help me to love her better, to love her as You love me. Remind me daily of Your design and purpose for my life. Use me to lead and serve my wife. I pray that she would be encouraged to be more like You, by the way I love her. Make my marriage show the world who You are.

In Jesus' name, AMEN!

Invite your wife to take a walk with you in nature to see God's incredible design up close.

STATUS UPDATE: @husbandrevolution Daily pursue a marriage that looks more and more like Christ and the church. #HusbandAfterGod

JOURNAL QUESTIONS:
How does your perspective of marriage change now that you know it was designed for a purpose?

What is one thing that makes it hard for you to love your wife like Christ?

What are some ways you can show your wife unconditional love?

LEAD BY EXAMPLE

Matthew 20:28, John 13:1-17, Ephesians 5:1,

Ephesians 5:25-30

The room was illuminated by candlelight. Jesus and His close friends reclined at the table together. The aroma of warm bread and wine filled the room with a sense of celebration, but not in the way the other men expected.

Jesus was about to go to the cross, He was about to suffer horribly, and yet His desire was to spend some of His last moments on Earth with His friends.

Motivated by love, Jesus took off His robe and tied a towel around His waist, then filled a bowl with water and began to go around the table taking hold of each of His disciples feet, one by one. He washed the dirt from their toes, ankles, and heels. The Creator of the universe humbly knelt before sinful men.

At this moment, Jesus provided an awesome example of strong leadership by becoming the servant of those He was entrusted with. After He was done washing their feet, He said to them,

"Now that I, Your Lord and Teacher, have washed your feet, you also should wash one another's feet."

You have been entrusted with the heart of your wife, and Christ has asked you to lead her the way He leads His church. Jesus did not put Himself above His disciples, neither should you put yourself and your needs above your wife. The powerful example Jesus gave you through His action of washing the disciples feet is an example of Jesus laying Himself down for the welfare of His disciples. In the same way, you must bend your heart in humility and serve your wife faithfully. You are called to lead your wife just like Jesus. "Washing her feet" means to care about her emotional, mental, and spiritual state; It means to help her in times of weakness, it means to carry her burdens, so she knows she is not alone, and it means being there for her when life gets messy as you walk through life alongside her.

Marriage is an opportunity to trudge through the mire with your wife, a journey that requires close contact. Serving your wife is done through sharing intentional words and intentional touch, both of which cultivate incredible intimacy.

Fulfilling your calling to lead her will deeply root confidence, hope, trust, and security in her heart and ultimately lead her closer to God. You are not only capable of loving and leading your wife this way; God requires you to do it, every single day of her life.

Just as Christ took the initiative to serve His disciple during dinner that night and in doing so set an example of how they must serve each other, so also you will be setting an example to your wife when you serve her first.

Whether or not she initiates in physical intimacy, going to church, participating in Christian fellowship, seeking godly counsel, reading the Bible, being forgiving, patient or even respectful, you should be willing to do these things first. Embrace the responsibility of leading your wife. Take the example of Christ and be an example for her. Being obedient to the Word of God is true spiritual leadership.

Dear Lord,

Thank You for giving me a perfect example of what it means to be a servant and to love like You love. Thank You for giving me an opportunity in my marriage to be obedient to Your words. Lord, give me a servant's heart for my bride. Give me strong hands to hold her up and gentle hands to care for her needs. I know it is time for me to stand up and spiritually lead my family by word and actions. Help me to do this by transforming my mind and heart from being selfish to selfless. I pray that my wife will see the difference in me as I begin to lead by example in my home. When my wife doesn't treat me the way I want to be treated I pray that You will give me the strength to continue to serve her without expectation.

In Jesus' name, AMEN!

Plan a date night at home with food and drink and have prepared what you need to wash your wife's feet. Read John 13:1-17 to your wife and share with her what God is teaching you and then wash her feet. Finish the night out with prayer.

STATUS UPDATE: @husbandrevolution I will embrace the responsibility of leading my wife and family just as Jesus leads the church. #HusbandAfterGod

JOURNAL QUESTIONS:

What do you think was going through the disciples minds as Jesus washed their feet?

Write a few things you can foresee happening if you began to lead you family like Christ.

List some more ways you can serve your wife in your everyday life.

YOUR SPOUSE IS A GIFT

Proverbs 18:22, Matthew 7:11, James 1:17

Perspective is powerful. How you perceive your wife will inevitably affect how you love her. Do you see her as your lover, your friend, your enemy, an inconvenience or maybe even a mistake? Over time, your experiences and circumstances throughout your marriage will begin to shape your perspective of your bride. The key is to allow God to be the one who shapes your perspective. You could allow all of the struggles and heartaches, the unmet expectations, the sin and everything else in between cause you to see your wife with jaded glasses or you can allow God to transform the way you see so that you can have a godly perspective of her and to continually see her for the gift that she is. Whether you can see it or not, your wife is a gift that God will use to bless you and refine you.

Have you ever looked at your wife as a gift, especially one from God? Gifts are always intended to be good things and God, your heavenly Father, gives the best gifts, and your wife is one. You may have a perspective that needs a drastic overhaul. It's time to receive your wife as the gift that she is. You need to take the time to unwrap your gift and get to know her well. As you become familiar with your gift, you will begin to see her value, and you will learn how to love her the way God desires.

Do not let a day go by without thanking God for her; by doing this your perspective will begin to shift to the right place.

God does not want you to feel disappointment as you open your gift; rather He desires that you discover all the complexities, beauty, and depth of your gift as you unwrap it daily. So if discontentment creeps into your heart about marriage, you must address it! You must remind yourself that marriage is an incomparable gift.

Do not forget so easily that God knows you better than you know yourself. When you grasp this truth, you will end up seeing your wife as the gift she is. A compliment, a companion, a counterpart. She is yours, and you are hers. Humbly receive your gift from God, trusting in His will for your life.

Once you begin to see your wife as the gift that she is and when you begin to walk in this truth you will then be in a place where the Lord can use your marriage in powerful ways. Your marriage is a ministry, where you and your wife have the opportunity to team up and bless others by praying for them, showing compassion, showing hospitality, and reflecting Christ's love as you mirror His image. Be a gift to others in this world. For it is in the heart that generosity and gratefulness push out discontentment.

The way that you live your life and the choices you

make, can have a profound impact on others, an impact that helps people turn their hearts to God with a positive perspective.

Dear Lord,

Thank You for Your goodness. Thank You that Your true character is not based on my perspective of You. You are the same yesterday, today and forever. You do give good gifts. Thank You for my gift. I am sorry that I have not seen my wife for the gift that she is. Forgive me for not seeing my marriage as a gift. I know now that You have given me my wife and marriage to lead me closer to You and to give me an opportunity to grow and change. Lord, You love me so much, and You always give good gifts. My wife is a good gift. My marriage is a good gift. Even in the hard times help me to see what this gift can bring. Lord, I also pray that my marriage would be a gift to this world. Use my marriage to bless others and to spread the Gospel. Use us Lord.

In Jesus' name, AMEN!

Be intentional about viewing your wife as a gift today. Treat her like the best gift you have ever received and thank God for her. If you struggle with your perspective of God or your wife, take a moment to pray.

STATUS UPDATE: @husbandrevolution My wife is a gift from God, and I will thank Him daily for her. #HusbandAfterGod

JOURNAL QUESTIONS:
What was your perspective of your wife when you were first married?

How does your attitude toward your wife reflect how you perceive God's gift?

What kind of things would your wife experience if you treated her as the gift she is?

SACRIFICIAL LOVE

Hebrews 10:14, 1 Timothy 2:6, John 14:6, Luke 9:23,
John 14:23, 2 Corinthians 5:17, 1 John 4:16

Betrayed by a close friend. Accused of wrongdoing. Sentenced to death. His body beaten, His character mocked, His Spirit crushed. Excruciating affliction and gaping lacerations, leaving Him unrecognizable. Despite the agony He was suffering, He continued to walk Himself to His death. Anguish gripped His heart, yet He persevered. Blood poured from His wounds, and He carried on. There was no rescue plan. This man knew what was to come. Still, He walked on, headed toward the place where He would breathe His last breath. His motivation was you.

Jesus Christ was sacrificed for you and all mankind. He endured harsh treatment and death on the cross, providing the world a way of redemption from sin, and His sacrifice remains the only way to be reconciled to God. He humbly walked that path, regardless of whether or not anyone accepted Him as Lord and Savior. He didn't do it because you deserve it or because you earned it. There is only one way He could have endured that immense amount of pain: true, unconditional, sacrificial love. The power of that kind of love transforms those who believe in it, drawing them closer to God. The closer you are to God, the more your character is transformed to be like His character. As you draw closer to God and spend time reading His Word, your life changes. You gain understanding and wisdom in who He is and how He operates. The Holy Spirit leads you through a journey of transformation. You leave your old ways and become a new creation. Your image begins to reflect His.

God's love is transforming. If you abide in God, His love is in you. With the One true God living in you, you will have the same power that Jesus walked in when heading to the cross. You will be able to love your wife with that same sacrificial love.

The power of this sacrificial love will transform your marriage.

You have the opportunity to express the sacrificial love of Christ toward your wife, not because she deserves it and not because she earns it, rather out of obedience to Christ and your love for her. Through the power of the Holy Spirit, your sacrificial and unconditional love will enable and motivate you to endure through any marital struggle, issue or circumstance, just like Christ endured for you.

Dear Lord,

I can't imagine what it must have been like for Jesus to go through what He went through on the cross. Thank You for this sacrifice so that I can have perfect and complete salvation in Your Son, Jesus. Lord, I pray that I will take up my cross daily in my marriage so that I will love my wife with a sacrificial love. I pray that I would put her needs above my own. May I love her when she is unlovable. May I forgive her when she has wronged and hurt me. Help us to endure together, no matter what we may face. Lord, have Your way in my marriage.

In Jesus' name, AMEN!

Consider what it means to love your wife with sacrificial, unconditional love. Make a list of what that looks like in your marriage. Then use this list as a reminder of how to love your wife this week.

STATUS UPDATE: @husbandrevolution I will have a sacrificial and unconditional love for my wife out of obedience to Christ. #HusbandAfterGod

JOURNAL QUESTIONS:

What do you think Jesus means when He tells us to take up our cross and follow Him?

What are some examples of sacrificial love in your marriage?

Where can you find the strength and motivation to love your wife especially when she doesn't deserve it?

What things tempt you to withhold your love from your wife?

BE RECONCILED

Romans 5:10, Romans 5:18-19, 2 Corinthians 5:17-20, Isaiah 55:6-7, Acts 8:22, Psalms 34:14, James 4:4, Colossians 3:13, Matthew 5:24

The actions of man are momentous and serious. Through one action came condemnation for all because of the choice to disobey God and bring sin into the world. Through another man's actions came freedom from sin, eternal life and the ministry of reconciliation.

Adam and Eve sinned in the Garden of Eden, severing their intimate bond with God. Although God never left them, they and all of humanity, now had enmity with God because of sin. God sought to reconcile His relationship with man through the death and resurrection of His Son, Jesus Christ. The sacrifice of Christ brought righteousness to all by the gift of grace, allowing everyone the opportunity to have an intimate relationship with God and spend eternity with Him.

God has given you the ministry of reconciliation, and He has committed to you the message of reconciliation through Christ. You are an ambassador of Christ to bring the good news of God's grace to others. However, you must be reconciled to God to be able to understand it and to share it with others. Reconciliation requires righteous action. It requires you to intentionally choose to believe and confess Christ, to repent of your sin and to obey God. In doing this, your life will reflect the grace you have received, thus becoming a minister of the Gospel.

As a believer who has been given the message of reconciliation with God, you must also be good at earthly reconciliation, such as between you and your wife. This requires you to extend God's grace to your wife, mirroring Christ's love despite circumstance or situation. Your role as a husband is a continuous opportunity to exercise and fulfill your call as an ambassador of Christ. Every action you make is momentous and serious. Every action you make will positively or negatively affect your wife. You will either be pointing her toward God or leading her away from Him. The choice is up to you.

The charge for you is to walk in humility. You should be bold to repent of your sins and to apologize when necessary, and to offer freely forgiveness to your wife as God has forgiven you. Restore harmony, peace, and oneness in your marriage. Remember, Christ did not wait for an apology from anyone before surrendering Himself in humility to make things right. No, He acted first. As a husband who has been reconciled to God through Jesus, you now have the power of reconciliation as you seek to restore your relationship with your wife at any sign of discord or sin. This is not an easy thing to do. Your pride will tempt you to withhold, your intellect will try to justify what is fair, your heart will attempt to manipulate your motives. However, through the victory that Christ has given you, you can choose to deny your flesh for the sake of reconciliation, for the sake of leading your wife in the Lord, this is a mark of a godly Husband.

Dear Lord,

Thank You for loving me so much even though I have sinned. Thank You for sending Your Son to reconcile me to yourself. If I have anything in me that needs to be repented of, then I repent. Open my eyes so that I am aware of my sin, so I can commit to not doing those things anymore. Take away anything in my life that is keeping me from a closer relationship with You. Lord, You have now given me this ministry of reconciliation, and I want to take the ministry seriously. Give me the strength to walk and live out this calling. I pray that I would always seek to reconcile with my bride as You did with me. I want my marriage to be a light of hope in this dying world. Lord, may You be glorified in our marriage.

In Jesus' name, AMEN!

Initiate reconciliation by apologizing for a sin and/or extending forgiveness to your wife, whether with a past offense or with the next disagreement or sin.

STATUS UPDATE: @husbandrevolution Always pursue reconciliation in marriage. #HusbandAfterGod

JOURNAL QUESTIONS:
How did God reconcile the world to Himself?

Write out your own definition of reconciliation.

What usually keeps you from mending your relationship with your wife after an argument or offense?

SET YOURSELF APART

Hebrews 10:10-12, Isaiah 55: 8, Colossians 2:6-7,
Romans 6:22, John 17:17, 2 Timothy 2:21,
2 Corinthians 5:17, Proverbs 17:3, 1 Peter 1:7,
1 Corinthians 6:11, John 16:33

God ingeniously provided many things here on Earth that reflect His love for us and the power of His testimony. God loves us too much to leave us slaves to our sin. Instead, He has given us grace and victory through His Son, Jesus Christ. You may be found a little rough around the edges. You may feel dirty or covered by your sin. You may even be familiar with hiding, not understanding your value or your purpose. Like gold found in the soil, you are found in the hands of the One who made you, the One with the key to victory.

Did you know that gold goes through a refining process? Raw gold is separated from the worthless rock and sand, cleaned up and then refined through fire. Fire is used to heat the gold to extreme temperatures, impurities rise to the surface and are then removed, a process repeated until the result is pure gold.

In this life you will go through fire; you will experience

hardships and trials and they will draw impurities to the surface of your heart. You will face things that will cause inner conflict as you learn to let go of your old ways while being transformed to live out God's ways.

Just as it is necessary for a skilled goldsmith to remove the impurities from the gold, God purifies you and His Holy Spirit sanctifies you. As the Holy Spirit leads you through each season of challenge and change, you will become more refined, pure, holy.

Sanctification means that you are set apart. When a person accepts Jesus as Lord and Savior, they are set apart from the rest of the world; they become a Christian--one who follows Christ. In this sense, sanctification occurs when you are saved in that by divine grace sins are covered, and forgiveness is granted. Sanctification is also defined as a process of transformation. As a Christian, you are set apart to be made holy.

Even though you are saved through grace, you have habits and characteristics from your old self that need to be transformed and made new by God. This produces an inner struggle of sin and holiness between your flesh and spirit. Although this conflict can be difficult to experience, the more you trust in God's ways and practice godliness, repenting of your sins and choosing not to practice sin, the more your character will reflect more of His.

You are a husband who made vows to your bride. Promising to no longer operate in selfishness, you now seek to lead, love and serve her. Your wedding was a memorable event where you entered into a covenant with your wife, setting yourself apart exclusively for her.

And, yet, marriage is also a process of transformation, learning how to adjust from your old ways of being single, to thinking of and living with another.

You will experience hardships, trials, and tests together. You will also face conflict between each other as both of your sin tendencies come to the surface. Marriage is a very powerful tool that God will use to bring the impurities in your flesh to the surface, but you will need to allow God to scrape them away once they do.

Over time, this journey you are on with your wife will grow and mature both of you. The changes you will experience, through the different seasons of marriage, will lead you to refinement if you choose to accept marriage as a way for God to transform you. The choice to embrace God's ways will always be up to you, and it will always begin by submitting yourself to Him and abiding in Him.

Dear Lord,

Thank You for freeing me from the bondage of sin and giving me complete victory through Your Son, Jesus Christ. Lord, I desire that my marriage would be set apart for Your glory and honor. I pray that I would humble myself so that You can use my marriage as a powerful tool to bring true and lasting refinement and change in my wife and me. I pray that I remember Your purpose for my marriage when we go through trials and hardship. I pray that I would recognize when You are drawing my sin to the surface so that I will allow You to scrape it away. Refine us and make us holy and set apart for You.

In Jesus' name, AMEN!

Take a good look at your wedding ring, a precious metal that endured refining fire and was crafted into a perfect, unending circle. Let it serve as a reminder that your marriage will encounter fire, but that if you surrender it to God it can withstand anything. When you look at your wedding ring, be reminded to pray for your marriage.

STATUS UPDATE: @husbandrevolution I will allow God to use my marriage to refine me. #HusbandAfterGod

JOURNAL QUESTIONS:
In what ways are you sanctified or "set apart" as a husband?

What transformations are you currently experiencing as a Christian or as a husband?

How can you respond to your wife differently knowing that the trials you face together have the potential to produce spiritual transformation in your marriage?

BE BRAVE

Joshua 1:9, Proverbs 28:1, 1 Corinthians 16:13,
Hebrews 12:7-14, 2 Timothy 1:7, 1 Peter 5:8,
Ephesians 6:12, 1 Timothy 6:12

You have been equipped by God to endure in this life. He has built you to be strong and courageous. He designed you with a spine to stand up for what is right, hands to work hard and provide, a mouth to speak His truth, a mind to make wise choices, a heart to love your wife unconditionally, and muscles to exercise your strength for the purpose of His will.

You are a warrior with the power, dwelling inside you, to live boldly and righteously.

In this life you will face many trials. Being brave is about being ready to face and endure any circumstance. Being brave is about being prepared both physically and spiritually to defend your faith and to protect your wife's heart. There will be people and situations that threaten these two things. You must be a man who is not distracted by selfishness, and you must not be a man entangled in sin. Otherwise, your adversary will blind side you in your weaknesses.

Be sober-minded so that you can critically think about your strategy that will lead to victory. You must resist the temptations of your flesh that tempt you to reject God's call on your life, and you must know God's truth so that you can rebuke the enemy's lies. Be brave and be bold in your actions when worshipping God and loving your wife. Be watchful over your marriage, quick to destroy any insecurity or doubt that makes you question if your marriage has an extraordinary purpose.

Being brave is about standing strong. Being brave is about remaining faithful when the world tells you there is no God, when the world mocks you for believing or having convictions to live a holy life, or when the world challenges what you know to be true. Being brave is about standing in faithfulness regardless of persecution.

Be faithful. Be faithful in your marriage, your job, your finances, your leadership, and in romancing your wife. Be faithful in your word, in your parenting, your friendships, and in how you use your social media.

You are a warrior. Be brave as you fight the good fight. For the struggle is not against flesh and blood, but against the spiritual forces of evil. Be a man of courage, for God is with you.

Dear Lord,

Make me brave and give me the courage to fight the good fight for my marriage and my faith. Give me a sober mind and teach me to stand strong against temptations. Lord, purify my heart and forgive me for my lack of strength. Give me endurance and power. Help me to protect my wife's heart and help me to stand with her in faith through every trial that comes our way. Make me courageous to speak and act in holiness. I pray against fear, depression, anxiety and anything else that will hinder me from living out Your will. I dedicate my life to You.

In Jesus' name, AMEN!

Be honest with your wife and ask her to be honest with you about fears that either of you may have and then use scripture to encourage each other away from fear.

STATUS UPDATE: @husbandrevolution I will always fight to protect my wife's heart. #HusbandAfterGod

JOURNAL QUESTIONS:

Do you feel strong or weak in your faith? Explain your answer.

Explain what it looks like to be brave in your faith and marriage?

What challenges do you face with being a brave husband when your wife doesn't respond the way you expect her too? Why should you do it anyways?

PROTECTING YOUR MARRIAGE

1 Timothy 5:8, Proverbs 25:26, Psalm 101, Ephesians 6:18,
1 Peter 5:8

The bus station was bustling with busy travelers and buses rushing to fill up passengers for the last few routes of the day. A husband and wife waited patiently for their bus to arrive.

Among the sea of people, a man made eye contact with the wife and overtly communicated his desire for her with a few winks, a nod of his head and pursed his lips together. The wife immediately felt uncomfortable and violated, as if the man was trying to undress her with his eyes. She grabbed her husband's arm and moved closer to him, fearing the motives of the strange man who made an advance at her. Her motion was swift, and her husband quickly assessed that something was wrong with his wife. He put his hand over her hand, but before he could ask what was troubling her, he looked out and saw for himself the other man walking toward them with aggression in his eyes and a perverse smile on his face. Although the wife feared any confrontation, it all happened too quickly for her to object.

Her husband jumped to his feet and yelled with a deeply stern tone in his voice, "Hey man, that's my wife. Leave her alone." The stranger could sense the threat from the husband without any more words being spoken. He turned his back from the couple, laughing with his friends as he walked away.

This world is full of evil and darkness in people. There will be times that strangers will attempt to take advantage of you and your wife. There will be times that acquaintances stir up strife. There will be times that family or close friends will emotionally attack one or both of you, and often times the fight will simply be between you and your wife.

For example, when intimacy issues arise and your wife is emotionally sensitive to what is happening, she may need a protector that can comfort her heart from pain and disappointment. Or perhaps when she is afraid for a particular reason, and she needs a protector to pray for her. Maybe she will wrestle with anxiety, and will need a protector to help her recognize what is triggering the anxiety and remind her of God's promises.

God has purposed you, as the husband, to be a protector of your wife's heart. You must be alert at all times, discerning situations that may require you to act in a righteous, yet forthright way. You will experience opportunities to encourage your wife while simultaneously being the one to confront issues and set boundaries that protect your wife and family.

A husband must always passionately and purposefully protect his wife's heart.

Although physically protecting your wife is extremely important there is another way that you must protect her. The spiritual atmosphere in your home is your responsibility to protect and cultivate. Be diligent to safeguard your marriage by not allowing anything into your home that may spiritually compromise it.

As your adversary prowls around and seeks ways to divide your marriage, be a husband who is willing to protect your marriage by being the one who cultivates unity and oneness with your wife. You can do this and protect your marriage by pursuing emotional, physical, and spiritual intimacy with your wife. Be willing to communicate with her daily. Be keenly aware of her needs and do what you can to fulfill them. Doing this protects your marriage from being vulnerable to the attacks of the enemy.

As you lead your wife spiritually, protect her by teaching her God's Word, which means you must know God's Word well enough to teach it. Keep her accountable to remaining faithful to spending intimate time with God daily. If you have children, do the same for them. Set an example that teaches them how to do this, by doing it yourself. Your personal relationship with God must be of utmost priority to you.

Be vigilant to consider everything you allow into your heart, mind, and home. Be sure that the music you are listening to, the content you are reading, what you expose yourself to on the internet, is pure. What you bring into your heart, you bring into your home. Are you allowing the enemy in, giving him access to your wife and family, or are you being vigilant to protect them?

Be intentional to know the condition of your relationship with God and the condition of your marriage. Be intentional to invest your time well. Be intentional to spend time gaining understanding in how you can best protect your heart and your wife's heart.

You are a warrior. You are a husband. Your purpose is to protect and love. Do it at all cost.

Dear Lord,

Forgive me if I have not protected my family physically and spiritually. Forgive me if I have allowed evil into my home either through media or my thoughts. I pray that from now on I would consider everything I do and say and evaluate if it is putting my family in physical or spiritual danger. I pray that I would do everything in my ability, through the power of the Holy Spirit, to protect my wife and children. Lord, help me have a passion to learn Your Word so that I can teach it to my wife and children. Put Your Word in my heart and let it keep me from anything that would hurt my marriage.

In Jesus' name, AMEN!

Consider an area of your life that your wife does not have access to and invite her into it. This could be a physical place, a bank account, a social media site, your phone or your email.

STATUS UPDATE: @husbandrevolution I will protect my marriage, physically and spiritually, at all cost. #HusbandAfterGod

JOURNAL QUESTIONS:
Are there any areas in your life that you are allowing danger into your marriage? What you watch, listen to, friends you hang around, etc…?

Is there any current situation that requires you to confront the issue and set a boundary?

In what way is God a protector and how does it make you feel knowing you were made in His likeness?

THE GOOD FIGHT

Galatians 6:9, 1 Timothy 6:11-12, Galatians 5:17,
Proverbs 8:13, Ecclesiastes 4:12, James 4:17, Mark 10:8,
1 Thessalonians 5:16-18, Titus 1:7-9, Philippians 4:4-9

Whether you realize it or not, you are in the midst of a spiritual battle. Your carnal flesh rages war against your spirit daily. Your flesh desires what is contrary to the Spirit, stirring up conflict within you.

In addition to your personal inner turmoil, consequences of the fall and repercussions of sin, the enemy seeks to devour your life, to ruin your marriage, and to destroy the testimony of Christ.

This is the fight; the daily tug-of-war between choices that determine whose side you are fighting for.

It can be easy to be distracted by believing the fight is with your wife. Do not be distracted in believing that winning a fight with your wife, or getting her to admit that you are right, is honorable or pleasing in any way to God. In fact, God hates pride, because pride keeps you from seeing things God's way. Pride will keep your heart hardened. When your heart is hardened, it is more susceptible to give into the temptations of the flesh.

When you give up and give in to your flesh, you sin. Sin is an immoral act, a transgression, an offense. Sin is always a choice. Sin is knowing what is good and not doing it. The immediate gratification you were seeking is shortly lived; what follows are a series of negative affects, and you are not the only one subject to them. You and your wife are one flesh, which means she is also affected by your poor choices.

When you sin, you are choosing to fight against God and against your wife. But God desires you to have self-control over your flesh and walk in the Spirit. Anyone who walks in the Spirit will honor God, and no longer gratifies the desires of the flesh.

Be above reproach. Choose to live life with a humble heart, one that is yielded to God. Be on guard. Be a man of God, a warrior of honor, fleeing from immorality in the pursuit of righteousness. Be a moral man who others can trust, especially your wife.

When you choose to walk in obedience to God, you choose to walk in victory. When you love and cherish your wife unconditionally, you will plant a seed of respect in your wife. When you repent of your sins, you will be set free. When you pray without ceasing, you will encounter God's transcending peace.

You vowed to be a husband. Fulfill your commitment by leading your wife in the good fight of faith by inviting her to pray with you, by meditating on God's Word together, by keeping her accountable and by affirming her in her relationship with the Lord. Spur her on toward righteousness and maturity. Fight alongside your wife, never against her. Invite God to be at the center of your marriage. Faithfulness to God will make you remain faithful to your wife.

Persevere, man of valor, when things get tough or when you lack understanding. Persevere. Do not grow weary in doing good and you will reap a harvest in your marriage.

Dear Lord,

I desire to walk in the Spirit and to honor You with my life and marriage. Forgive me of my sins and teach me to walk in righteousness. Lord, I will no longer allow my pride to get in the way of oneness with my wife. I will stop fighting with my wife and start fighting alongside my wife. Fighting for peace, hope, faith and righteousness. I will pray with my wife, I will meditate on the Word with my wife, I will seek after Your kingdom first with my wife. Lord, be the center of my marriage. Help me to persevere and not grow weary of doing good. Help me to keep worshiping You even when things are hard in my life and marriage. Help me to keep loving my wife even when it is hard.

In Jesus' name, AMEN!

When you find yourself beginning to fight with your wife, stop and remember that your wife is not your enemy and that you are on the same side. Be humble and then ask if you can pray about the issue together.

STATUS UPDATE: @husbandrevolution I will not grow weary in doing good for my wife. #HusbandAfterGod

JOURNAL QUESTIONS:
What are some examples of your flesh and your spirit fighting against each other?

In what ways have you witnessed your sin negatively affecting your marriage?

What is one area of your life where you are fighting the good fight of faith, resisting sin and honoring God?

GOD'S ECONOMY

Malachi 3:10, Proverbs 6:9-11, Matthew 6:21,
Romans 12:1-2, Romans 13:8, 1 Timothy 6:6-10, 2
Corinthians 9:7, Philippians 4:19

A husband rushed home from work, eager to search the mail for good news. The door squeaked open and his wife turned toward her husband with excitement. With mail in one hand, the husband reached his other arm around his wife and greeted her with a firm hug.

"Is it here?" she asked her husband.

They had been waiting anxiously for the confirmation letter that would change their life dramatically. He replied with a grin on his face, holding up the envelope,

"Yup!" He sat down at his desk and quickly opened the letter.

His wife cried and laughed at the same time, hugging her husband with joy exploding from her heart, "We did it, Honey! We are debt-free!"

For two years, this couple prayed and asked God to wipe

away their debt. They worked full-time jobs and gave up their weekends to work toward their financial goals, usually putting a thousand dollars or more each month to pay off the balance owed. Their journey did not lack situations where they sacrificed their wants and desires to meet these goals. It also did not lack moments when they got angry with one another, arguing over money. Regardless of how difficult their financial situation was, they remained faithful to God, tithed regularly, and trusted in God's economy more than in the world's economy.

The world promotes a debt-filled lifestyle. The pressure to use and rely on credit cards, loans and other forms of risky investments is extremely high. The world's economy fluctuates, inflates, crumbles. The negative affects and implications of living with debt is a force of destruction for every marriage and family.

The enemy will tempt you with desires of your heart and try to convince you to believe that the world's economy is secure. The truth is that the only security you will ever find is in God alone.

God wants you to trust Him with your family, with your living situation, with your job, with your wallet, with everything. As you trust in God and as you lead your family according to His ways, you will have everything you need, including contentment. God's ways are found throughout His Word. If you desire to lead your family, you must know God's Word.

In God's economy, the biggest risk for you is never saying, "Not my will, Lord, but may Your will be done." The truth is that you will gain everything you will ever need by saying and believing these words.

If you want to love God and love your wife faithfully, you must assume the responsibility to be a good steward of what God has given to you. This includes caring for your wife, having a strong commitment to work, faithfully giving generously to God, giving generously to others in need, managing your budget, and owing nothing to anyone, but love.

Trusting in God and carrying out His ways requires a sound mind, a cheerful attitude, and a hopefulness about the future. Lead your wife in your finances, lead her to trust in God's security, pray about purchases without rushing to buy, be wise, have self-control and live within your means. The joy that you and your wife will experience when you pursue God and trust in Him with your lives is immeasurable.

Dear Lord,

I submit my finances to You. I surrender my control over them and ask that You would guide me by Your Holy Spirit. Give me a heart that desires to give to You the tithe that You ask for. Lord, give me a heart to be more generous with those around me that are in need. May I not trust in the world's economy, but rather trust completely in You and Your provision for my life. I ask for wisdom in the area of money, and I ask that You would guide us into a debt free mindset. I pray that we would one day only have an outstanding debt of love to one another. Please help us to be a debt-free family!

In Jesus' name, AMEN!

CHALLENGE:
Trust God with your finances this week. Whether or not it is in your budget, pray about how much you want to give back to God and faithfully give it to Him.

STATUS UPDATE: @husbandrevolution I will be content and trust in the Lord's provision for my life. #HusbandAfterGod

QUESTIONS:
What challenges do you face in trusting God with tithing regularly?

What can you initiate and implement today to get your family debt free?

Do you trust God will take care of you or are you fearful?

THE ARMOR OF GOD

Ephesians 5:33, 1 Timothy 2:1-6, Matthew 6:24, Ephesians 6:1-4, Ephesians 6:10-18, Hebrews 4:12, 2 Corinthians 5:21

A soldier is a skilled warrior, equipped and trained for combat. You are a soldier in God's army. You are a warrior. You are equipped by God to fight against the dark forces of this world, your enemy is the devil. The battle is real and it is happening right now. The battle is a spiritual war over souls. God desires that all men are saved, yet the enemy seeks to kill, steal and destroy. A man cannot serve two masters. Every day is an opportunity to serve God and worship Him, or to serve yourself and to worship the enemy.

Are you prepared to fight?

A soldier is very intentional about being prepared for combat. Protective gear, weapons, strategy, strength, and power are necessary for victory.

God has given you everything you need to be prepared as a soldier in His army. The armor of God is outlined in His Word and with it you will defeat the enemy, thwarting his advances against you, against your marriage and against God's Kingdom.

It is no coincidence that the armor of God is detailed in scripture immediately after the mention of family relationships. God was intentional about its placement, knowing that the utmost intimate relationships would be a continuous target for the enemy's attacks. It is imperative that you heed God's wisdom and suit up, for the sake of your marriage, your family, and the testimony of Christ.

Belt of Truth - First and foremost, you must believe God's truth--His Holy Word. When you are feeling attacked, offended, stressed out or tempted, God's truth is the only comfort that will bring you healing and peace. You need to have a firm foundation in your heart of what God says about you. When hard times press in, let His unchanging truth keep you stable. The other part of this piece of armor is being a man of your word. Truthfulness is having sincerity in your actions and your character. Truth is doing what you say you will do and being honest with your words. If you tell your wife you will fulfill a need of her's at a certain time; you must follow through with your promise. By doing so, you build a reputation of truthfulness and trust with your wife. Truth in marriage creates a safe place for intimacy to increase.

Breastplate of Righteousness - The only true way to attain righteousness is to be in Christ. (2 Corinthians 5:21) As you submit to Christ in obedience, your character will be transformed to reflect His. The motivation to strive toward living a moral life comes from deep within your heart as your relationship with God develops.

The breastplate protects the heart. Likewise, you can protect your heart from the destruction and havoc of sin by choosing to live according to God's law. This is a daily choice you make when confronted with all kinds of decisions. By choosing righteousness, you are saying yes to love, joy, peace, patience, kindness, goodness, faithfulness, gentleness, and self-control. Such fruitfulness is required to enable your marriage to thrive.

Gospel of Peace – The good news of Christ's testimony comes with the power of transcending peace. Only He can truly fill your heart with peace in any situation you are facing. If you ever feel the weight of anxiety, depression, anger, fear, being overwhelmed, insecurity, unworthiness, or any other oppression that can so easily debilitate, you must lean on Him to receive the power of His peace. There is nothing you can do to set yourself free, and there is nothing your wife can do to make the oppression go away. Only God's peace can bring you healing and freedom. So when the pressure builds and the enemy advances, be prepared to rely on God for peace. Having the readiness of peace also means that you pursue harmony no matter where you are and no matter what your circumstance. Peace is especially vital to pursue in marriage. When you seek to be a peacemaker, selfishness diminishes while love builds up.

Shield of Faith – Faith is trusting in God, believing that His plans are best. In faith, you believe that God's plan for you and your wife is better than anything you can ever imagine because you know God's love for you both is great. Faith is also having confidence in things hoped for. If you hope to experience passionate intimacy with your wife, you must be confident in her ability to love you. If you hope to see your wife respect you as a God-fearing man, you need to be confident in your ability to lead her and lead her well. If you hope to share an awesome marriage with your wife, you should use your shield of faith to block any negativity from others, words that have the potential to put doubt in your heart. This will help you remain loyal to your wife and faithful to the hope you had when you first married her. Faith and hope feed your soul passion and purpose, which are elements needed to enjoy life and fight the good fight.

HELMET OF SALVATION – Salvation is defined as deliverance from sin and preservation from destruction. Just as God extended grace to you, be diligent in extending grace to your wife for her sin, faults, and failures. Deliver your wife from weakness through forgiving her, praying for her, and giving her the opportunity to change. Be mindful that neither you nor your wife are perfect, both of you are in need of daily grace. Preserve your marriage from destruction by investing in your marriage through gaining knowledge. Seek marriage resources that will enlighten your perspectives, inspire your passion, and challenge you to be transformed into the husband God desires you to be.

SWORD OF THE SPIRIT - One of your most powerful weapons of defense will always be the Word of God. The Sword of the Spirit is the powerful Word of God, which is living and active, sharper than any double-edged sword. (Hebrews 4:12) With God's Word you can learn how to live as He has called you to, you can learn about His truths, you can learn about His testimony, and you can learn about how to invest in your marriage. The Bible has power in it! Read it, memorize it, meditate on it, and lean on it for understanding. By actively utilizing the Bible, your faith will grow, you will be transformed and your marriage will be blessed as you are transformed into a God-fearing husband.

Along with all of the different pieces of armor, you are also encouraged to pray. Faith enables you to pray; to communicate with God, your Commander, your King. Through prayer, you can give thanks, and you can implore protection over your wife and family. Prayer is a powerful way to keep your life, your marriage, and your family focused on God.

God's Word exposes the reality of spiritual warfare, revealing to you the power you have to stand against evil forces. As a warrior of faith, you are called to action. God is calling you to put on the armor and not just pieces of it...the full armor of God! Make it part of your daily routine, dressing spiritually to prepare you for the battle at hand. Your marriage and your family depend on you!

Dear Lord,

Thank You for giving me the armor I need to have victory in my life and marriage. Lord, help me to walk in truth in every aspect of my life and remove any falsehood from my lips. May I strive toward righteousness as You are righteous. Make me a peacemaker for I want to be called a son of God. Give me a faith that is unmovable so that I can be an example for my wife and children. Thank You for the salvation You have given to me through Your Son, Jesus Christ. Put a passion for Your Word in me and write Your Word on my heart so that I will know Your ways and understand Your will. I love You Lord, and I desire to seek You out in prayer everyday, for myself, for my wife, and for my kids.

In Jesus' name, AMEN!

Memorize all the different pieces of the armor of God and talk to your wife about the importance of armoring up daily.

STATUS UPDATE: @husbandrevolution I will put on the full armor of God for my marriage. #HusbandAfterGod

QUESTIONS:
Write down each piece of armor and describe what they look like practically.

Why is it important for you to put on the full armor of God?

What could some of the "flaming arrows of the evil one" look like in your marriage?

PRIDE

Proverbs 8:13, Proverbs 11:2, Proverbs 13:10,
Proverbs 16:5, Proverbs 16:18, Mark 7:14-23 , 1 John 2:16,
Romans 12:3, Matthew 18:4

Pride swells up and makes a man think of himself more highly than he ought to, a breeding ground for self-deception. Pride is when you give weight to the things you have done and accomplished, convinced you did it all on your strength.

The message of pride settling in your heart says, "No one contributed, no one helped me do it, God didn't give me the strength or skill. I did it, and I want all the glory."

Pride believes that you are always right. Pride screams, "I must win." It declares your way as the best way. Pride is being focused on yourself, consumed with yourself, what you did, what you deserve, what you desire. Pride motivates the belief that it's all about you.

Pride is destructive to your marriage. Acting on pride is dangerous because its goal is self-preservation, not oneness.

Pride will make it impossible to love your wife through acts of kind service, because you will want to be served. It will challenge you in the midst of an argument with your wife, pressuring you to avoid reconciliation. It holds fast to the facts and adds up the math of a situation. Pride is about proof and results and who is right, all the while your wife just wants to know that you care about her and the condition of your marriage. It will also convince you to refrain from repenting until your wife repents, confesses or is caught first. It will cause you to bring her down to your level of shame so that you don't feel as bad. These postures, or attitudes of the heart, make it impossible to experience true intimacy with your wife. Rather, it has a polarizing effect, pushing her away.

A prideful heart has an extremely hard time exercising humility. A prideful heart does not know how to surrender in love.

God hates pride! Pride will deceive you into believing that you don't need Him. Pride keeps you from being humble, it keeps you from admitting when you have sinned, it keeps you from praying and it keeps you from leaning on God's truth. A heart full of pride is unteachable; therefore, the process of transformation is hindered. Pride quenches the Holy Spirit, severing your union with God. Pride is not motivated by love, it will keep you from surrendering, it will keep you from apologizing, and it will keep you from forgiving. Pride gives birth to bitterness and resentment. Without reconciliation, a husband and wife are wounded fatally. Pride will cause you to fall and it will destroy you.

If you want an intimate relationship with God and with your wife, you must resolve in your heart and mind to be humble. You need to repent of pride and choose to submit to God. You need to be sensitive to God's direction, you need to yield to His ways, you need to be aware of other's around you, and you need to be love-focused. If you want a thriving relationship with God and your wife, you must let go of your pride.

Dear Lord,

Forgive me for any pride that is in my heart. Forgive me if pride has kept me from You. Forgive me if my pride has hurt my wife. Lord, go into my heart and find any prideful way that I have and remove it far from me. Give me a humble heart and spirit. Lord, I don't want my pride to cause me to fall, I want to stand strong. I pray that You would help me reconcile any relationship where my pride has made a negative impact. I pray I would be love-focused. I pray I would be a man who walks humbly in every way.

In Jesus' name, AMEN!

Pray every day this week that God would reveal any pride that is in your heart. Write down the things that He reveals to you and then pray and work toward humbling yourself in those areas. Repent of that pride.

STATUS UPDATE: @husbandrevolution I lay down my pride so that I can have a blessed marriage. #HusbandAfterGod

QUESTIONS:
What do you think of when you hear the word pride?

Have you experienced pride in your heart and then experience a fall or a fight in your relationship with your wife because of it?

What is one thing you have been very prideful about recently and what do you feel God is calling you to do about it?

FORGIVENESS

Colossians 3:12-14, Matthew 18:21-35, 1 Peter 4:8,
Matthew 6:15

One of the scariest statements Jesus ever made can be found in Mark 6:14-15, "For if you forgive others their trespasses, your heavenly Father will also forgive you, but if you do not forgive others their trespasses, neither will your Father forgive your trespasses."

Consider these words deeply and understand the implications that they hold. As a follower of Christ, you have chosen to love and obey your Savior. His words hold more weight than any other in your life. When you said yes to Jesus, you immediately gave up your right to certain things, the most important being the choice to forgive others. You have forfeited the right to hold onto wrongdoings against you. The world will tell you that unless a person who has wronged you asks for forgiveness and changes their ways, you are not responsible for forgiving them. However, that is not what Jesus has taught in His Word.

Jesus makes it very clear to His disciples the significance of forgiveness. Jesus also gives a stern warning in

Matthew 18:21-35, take a moment to read it again. There is nothing that anyone in this world, especially your wife, can do to you that is more unworthy of forgiveness then what God forgive you for through His Son, Jesus. So, if you hold anyone in unforgiveness, you are effectively saying that what they did to you is worse than what you did to God. If you can have complete forgiveness, than so can others.

Forgiving your wife will not be easy. She will offend you at times, and in her weakness she will sin. Likewise, there will be times that you offend her and sin. Marriage is vulnerable because it is an intimate union between two sinners. The personal struggles you and your wife have will negatively impact one another and the quality of your marriage.

Without forgiveness, ruin in your relationship is inevitable.

There are many issues that can cause conflict in marriage including: finances, manipulation, lying, lust, pride and the list goes on. However, you and your wife are responsible for protecting your relationship against these sources of contention. One of the most powerful ways you can transform these conflicts into milestones of growth is through reconciliation.

Reconciliation is a result and culmination of apology and forgiveness, both of which require humility. Apology and forgiveness are vital and true signs of a healthy marriage. Do your part to keep your marriage strong through the willingness of practicing forgiveness.

Christ urges you to continue to forgive just like God

continues to forgive you. You can forgive because God's love has been poured into your heart through the Holy Spirit! As you choose to forgive your wife, you experience the power and authority derived from God!

Protect your marriage through repentance and forgiveness. Your response to sin is not contingent on how your wife reacts; rather you are commanded by and accountable to God to love your wife, unconditionally. Love covers sin. Protect your marriage by forgiving your wife, just as God forgives you, and encourage your wife not to give up when sin leads to shame or negatively affects your marriage, encourage her to hold on and hope.

Dear Lord,

I am sorry for the times that I have withheld forgiveness from my wife. I repent of my unforgiving heart and ask You to replace it with one that is full of grace and forgiveness. Lord, You have forgiven me of so much, and I don't deserve forgiveness. Help me to take that mercy and grace and use it as a reminder of how to love and forgive my wife and others. I pray bitterness would never settle in my heart. I pray against the temptation to justify unforgiveness. May Your grace abound in my relationships and most importantly in my marriage.

In Jesus' name, AMEN!

Lean on God for the power to forgive others, trusting in Him to heal you. If you have any unforgiveness towards your wife go to her and reconcile.

STATUS UPDATE: @husbandrevolution Repentance and forgiveness are vital and true signs of a healthy marriage. #HusbandAfterGod

QUESTIONS:
How does it make you feel when you consider the words of Jesus in Mark 6:14-15?

What things make it difficult to forgive your wife?

Is there anything you could forgive your wife for currently? Is there anything that you need to confess and ask forgiveness for?

ANGER

Psalm 7:11, 2 Kings 17:18, Romans 1:18, James 1:19-25, Ephesians 4:26, Proverbs 29:11, Proverbs 15:1, Colossians 3:8, Proverbs 25:28

God has given man a variety of powerful emotions, anger is one of them. God Himself knows anger very well.

God has given you the ability to feel anger so that you have a profound understanding of His heart and the things that matter to Him. It is okay to feel angry. However, God does command you not to sin in your anger.

There is a balance and boundary that needs to be upheld when it comes to expressing anger. This boundary needs to be put in place because of your flesh. Without self-control and restraint, your flesh would have the power to give full vent to its anger, which is unwise and very dangerous. When your flesh feels anger, it wants to physically exert it from the inside out. If you give full vent to your anger, allowing it to control you, you risk hurting yourself and others, especially your wife. Unrighteous anger can and will destroy your marriage.

Your flesh will want to use anger to justify yourself when you feel wronged or are agitated. Giving into your flesh in your anger severes unity with your wife because you are no longer operating as one flesh. When you act out of your anger unrighteously you no longer are protecting and defending your marriage, rather you pridefully pull yourself apart from your wife, stirring up all kinds of strife.

There are many men who are full of anger, yet do not comprehend its power. They misuse it and as a consequence abuse others with it. People use anger to scare, to threaten, to show superiority, to prove strength, to get a point across, to hurt, to weaken, to manipulate, to gain control, and to retaliate.

The Bible teaches the contrary; to be slow to get angry, to love one another, to be an ambassador of peace.

The necessary and righteous boundary for anger is exercising self-control to bridle your anger and direct its energy under the authority of God. The only way to formulate such a boundary and be subject to God is to turn your heart toward God in humility.

You must use your anger for good, to fight for the injustices in the world that matter to God. This includes defending your marriage. However, if you are distracted by getting easily angered by your wife and fighting with her, you will not have the capacity to simultaneously fight for her.

Reign over your emotions. Exercise self-control and implore God to help you, so that you do not sin when you are angry. Direct your energy toward the injustices of the world, the innocent being taken advantage of, the women being abused, the children being neglected, the marriages being destroyed, and so on.

Let God be your avenger, to act as He sees fit.

Dear Lord,

Take hold of my spirit and subject it to Yours. Teach me to have full control over my anger so that I will not sin against You or my wife. Forgive me of my anger. Lord, I pray that I would please You with my attitude and the words that I speak. Give me a heart that fights for Your causes. I pray I would have passion to serve You and fight for the injustices of the world as You want me to. I pray I would have self-control of my anger and that I direct its energy appropriately. Please show me how to be slow to get angry, especially with my wife. I pray for freedom from anger.

In Jesus' name, AMEN!

The next time you feel angry with your wife, pause and pray. Take time to navigate your anger and process them before responding to the situation. Make sure that you do not sin in your anger. Also, consider what things trigger your anger and ask God to transform you so that you are not easily angered by these triggers.

STATUS UPDATE: @husbandrevolution The anger of man does not produce the righteousness of God.#HusbandAfterGod

QUESTIONS:

What are some situations that trigger your anger?

What capacity of destruction does anger have in your life?

What are some actions you can take to make sure you have control over your anger?

LOVE HER

Ephesians 5:25-33, 1 Corinthians 13:4-8, Romans 13:8-10, 1 John 4:8, 1 Peter 3:7

You have been commanded to love your wife, but you will never be able to fulfill this commandment by accident. Loving your wife as Christ loves the church is a daily and conscious decision. Furthermore, to make the choice to love, you must know what love is.

The world and our enemy has taken every opportunity to define love by twisted and perverted standards. However, love is not defined by our enemy or the world, no, love is defined by God Himself and His definitive Word. To know how to love, you must first know God, because God is love.

Love is being patient with your wife. It is having the self-control to not exasperate her or stress her out. Love is being kind in your attitude, your actions, and your words. It means you do not get jealous of your wife or over your wife's relationships. It is communicating to her without pride.

Love is putting your wife's needs above your own. It

means you are not easily provoked by her, but rather respond to her in a way that reflects God's character. It means you are patient, kind, and tenderhearted toward her. It means you do not hold onto past sins of hers that can be used as ammunition in the midst of a heated conversation or disagreement. Love forgives her when she is wrong, repents when you are wrong, and strives to continue with intimacy and oneness regardless of how you may have hurt one another.

Love always protects your wife, always trusts in her, always hopes in her, always perseveres with her. Love never fails and love never gives up on her.

Love is cherishing your wife by romantically pursuing her. To love her means you pursue what would fill her heart with joy, what would feed her spirit, what would help her to know you want and desire her, and what would make her feel secure in your marriage. Loving your wife is knowing how to comfort her, how to listen to her, how to take the time to understand her and validate her feelings. Loving your wife means you wash her with the Word of God. Teaching, sharing, and discussing God's Word with her. Loving your wife means praying for her and with her daily.

Being present in your marriage and family is the first step to being able to love your family. Be there with them, more than you're not. If you can't be present because of work, then make sure you are in daily communication via phone, email or Skype.

Loving your wife will at times be inconvenient to your flesh. Love her anyways. Loving your wife will at times not make sense because she hurt you. Love her anyways. Loving your wife will at times be a challenge because she does not respond to it the way you expect. Love her anyways. When your marriage feels broken, love her anyways.

If you want to be like Jesus, you must love like Him. Real love is not a feeling. It's much greater than that. Unconditional love is a choice. With every action, you will prove whether you love your wife. Your love will promote and contribute to a healthy, thriving, God honoring marriage. It will be extremely hard for a wife not to respect and submit to her husband when he loves her like this.

Loving your wife means that you refuse to neglect her, that you put her needs above your own, that you never stop pursuing her and that you are always willing to get to know her intimately.

God directly commanded you as her husband to love her just like Christ loves the church. No other man on Earth can fulfill this for your wife. Be there for her and fulfill the need in her heart to be truly loved and completely cherished.

Above all else, always choose love.

Dear Lord,

Thank You for loving me with an everlasting love. Thank You for displaying that love to me long before I did anything in response to it. Teach me to love like this. Teach me to love like Your Son. My wife is a gift from You and I will love her as the best gift I have ever received. Give me creativity in the ways I can pursue her romantically. Give me the strength to hold her up when she is tired. Give me eyes to see when she needs my attention. Give me ears to hear her heart. Give me the words to speak life into her. Help me to choose love even when things get hard.

In Jesus' name, AMEN!

Memorize Ephesians 5:25-33

STATUS UPDATE: @husbandrevolution I will love my wife like Christ loves His church.#HusbandAfterGod

QUESTIONS:
Why do you believe God commanded husbands to love their wives like Christ?

How would your wife respond if you began to love her in this way?

What do you struggle with most when it comes to loving your wife?

WISDOM

Genesis 3:6, Proverbs 2, Proverbs 9:10,
1 Corinthians 1:18-31, James 1:5,
Proverbs 3:13, Proverbs 8

The heart of man desires to be recognized as wise. The pride of humanity says, "I know!" Yet, there are many who lack wisdom. Why is this so? Because wisdom is much more than knowledge.

Wisdom is the application of knowledge. If you "know" but you do not "do" than you are not wise. Wisdom is knowledge of what is right and acting justly in that knowledge. Foolishness is knowing the truth and doing nothing or doing the opposite. Foolishness is choosing to remain apathetic in your love relationship with your wife. Foolishness is being inactive and absent.

The Bible is clear about where wisdom comes from. Wisdom begins with the fear of God, and the Bible says He is the One who gives wisdom generously. Fearing God is shown through your actions in the way that you reverence Him, gestures motivated by deep respect for Him. For example, if you claim to know what God's Word says, but you don't do it, you are operating in foolishness.

Have you ever thought you were wise, confident that your way was the right way, yet you disregarded God's truth? Simply hearing God's Word doesn't make a wise man wise, but obeying God, abiding in Him, and doing what His Word says are the marks of a wise man.

To be a husband who effectively protects his marriage and family, you must be wise. With wisdom comes good judgement, discernment and the confidence to make choices that will honor God and bless your family. Meditate on Proverbs 2 and consider all the ways you can actively pursue wisdom. Know God's Word, listen up, apply it. Work hard to search for it and you will find it.

Pursue goldly wisdom, not the wisdom of the world. God's wisdom lacks nothing and the wisdom of the world is merely foolishness. If you desire wisdom, ask God, and He will give it to you generously. If you hunger for discernment and understanding, open a Proverb a day and study the power of God's wisdom exemplified through the testimony of Christ. As you strive to be more like God, repenting of sin and obeying His Word, you will gain wisdom and will be transformed because of it. This wisdom will be a blessing to you and your family.

Dear Lord,

I desire wisdom. Put fear in my heart for You. Fill me with Your truth and understanding. Lord, I want to lead my family in Your wisdom. I see now that I cannot continue on in my own wisdom. I pray that I would seek your face in every situation and would yield my life to Your will. Fill me with godly wisdom and give me the strength to act in the truth of Your Word. Help me to apply Your Word to my life whenever I make a decision, great or small. Help me to be a man of knowledge, wisdom, and understanding. Help me comprehend profound things. Make me intelligent and make me wise.

In Jesus' name, AMEN!

Evaluate your marriage and write down any areas that you feel you need more wisdom. Pray over this list fervently and make notes when God gives you wisdom in these areas.

STATUS UPDATE: @husbandrevolution To be a husband who effectively protects his marriage and family, I must walk in godly wisdom. #HusbandAfterGod

QUESTIONS:

In what instances have you acted on your wisdom instead of God's wisdom?

What are some areas in your life that you desire to have more wisdom?

How will being devoted to gaining God's wisdom affect your marriage?

WORDS MATTER

Ephesians 4:29, Proverbs 18:21, Proverbs 16:24, James 3,
Matthew 12:33-37, Psalm 19:14, Colossians 3:8,
Proverbs 12:18, Luke 6:45, Matthew 4:4

God cares about words. He invented them. He also used words to create the entire world and universe. The reason God cares about words is because they are powerful. Your tongue, although it is one of the smallest muscles you have in your body, is one of the most powerful tools guiding your life. The impact of your words can last through generations.

Humans have been communicating thoughts and ideas with one another using words since the beginning of time. Communication is a gift God has given to you so that you may express yourself and connect with others. As a husband and as the leader of your home, you have a responsibility to protect and provide a safe environment for authentic communication to take place. You and your wife should give each other mutual freedom to share with each other what matters to you both.

However, in your freedom, you must remember that your words matter. Not just your words, but also how you present those words. The tone in your voice, your body language and the attitude motivating your words, all matter.

The tongue has the power to bring life and death.

Are your words motivated by a deep love? Or are your words produced by the poison of bitterness and anger residing in your heart?

With your words, you can either build your wife up or tear her down. The choice to use your words for those two different purposes has been entrusted to you. God's Holy Word compares the tongue to a bit inside of a horse's mouth and the rudder of a ship, explaining how although small, the tongue directs the path of a man. The Bible also shares a warning, comparing the tongue to a fire; one small spark has the potential to burn down an entire forest. Your words have that same power.

Your words are also a reflection of what your heart already believes. Imagine your words flowing from your heart out through your mouth. You make known what is in your heart every time you speak. And being sarcastic, followed by "I'm just kidding" does not cover up the truth. Before you can change the direction and purpose of your words, you must first change what is in your heart.

Only God can help you change your heart through the process of transformation. The closer you draw to God, the better control you will have over your words. The closer you draw to God, your heart will be refined, which means your words will be refined. As you pursue righteousness in this way, your words will reflect a heart after God's heart, and that is powerful!

If you desire to be a man of life-giving words, you must know the Word, you must be in the Word, you must believe in the Word, and you must be wise and apply the Word.

Your marriage and the legacy you establish, in the authority of God, will be fueled by the words you speak, and how you speak them to your wife and children.

Be willing to communicate in a gentle, caring and understanding way. Be a husband who listens without distraction, who uses his words to comfort and heal, who enjoys intimately talking about the deep and serious matters. Let your words be a source of life to your wife, a minister of God's abiding love.

Dear Lord,

Search my heart and see if there is any malice in me. See if anger or strife has filled my heart. Cut any dead flesh away and renew in me a right spirit. Let the words of my mouth and the meditation of my heart be acceptable in Your sight, my Rock and my Redeemer. May I always think before I speak. Purify my lips. I pray others are blessed by my speech. I pray my wife is blessed through the words I speak to her. May my words reveal to my wife the love I have for her in my heart. Refine me and refine the content of my speech. Transform me from the inside out. Use me to be a man who gives life through his words.

In Jesus' name, AMEN!

Take a moment today to share with your wife why you are thankful for her. You can say it, you can write it in a letter, you can text it or any other form of communicating with her that will get her your message.

STATUS UPDATE: @husbandrevolution My words can bring life or death and I will chose to bring life with them to my wife. #HusbandAfterGod

QUESTIONS:

Do your words give your wife life or do they tear her down?

Why is it important to be responsible for your words?

In what ways can your words strengthen your marriage?

CALLED OUT

---

1 Peter 1:15-16, 1 Corinthians 6:12-20, Matthew 22:37-40, Galatians 1:15, Psalm 4:3, 1 Peter 2:9, Romans 12:2

Jesus picked each one of the men who would be His disciples. He invited them to participate in His ministry and to follow Him. Jesus traveled with these men, taking time in different locations to preach the truth of God. Jesus didn't call these men to follow Him so that He could have some travel buddies; He called them so that He could change them and make them into disciples. He took the opportunity to call them out on their disbelief, their sin, and even their attitudes. Jesus loved them, so He called them out.

There are people in this world who do not like being called out by God. When it happens they are offended, they give way to their anger, they complain, they justify their behavior, and they fight for their fleshly desires. They war against Jesus and His teachings because they do not want to submit to God. The culture of this world is spiraling out of control, raising up a generation who is turning its back to God.

With the inevitable pressures in this world capable of

bearing down on you to the point of exhaustion and even persecution, it is crucial that you confidently know who you are called to be according to your Maker, your God, your source of strength. He reveals who you are called to be throughout His Word.

You are His son and an heir, adopted through the resurrection of Christ. He knows you by name, and He has called you to be His.

He guides you to be a faithful man who upholds biblical standards of truth. As you read through the Word of God, you will start to recognize the specific callings that God has for you.

HERE ARE A FEW:
- You are called to be a provider. (1 Timothy 5:8)
- You are called to be a man of the Word. (Psalm 1:1-6)
- You are called to be the head. (Ephesians 5:23)

These are just three of the many examples mentioned in God's Word of who you are called to be. Each calling serves as a guide to help you define who God created you to be. Understanding who God calls you to be and intentionally living to fulfill each call will grow you closer to God, especially as you search His Word and meditate on it.

Your relationship with your wife will also deepen and strengthen as you are transformed in Christ and grow in His likeness. Your wife will be blessed through the godly changes occurring in your actions, attitudes, and words. Don't hesitate to explore who God calls you to be, and don't hesitate to answer the call by accepting His truth and acting in wisdom to live dedicated to all that He has commanded. Know the ten commandments and know the teaching of Christ.

It is also vital that you do not attempt to isolate yourself from the fellowship of faithful community. Invite God-fearing men to be your friend, to walk out this life with you. Ask them to keep you accountable to your faith, marriage and family. Give them permission to call you out on your behavior and any sin they see in your life. Sharpen one another, encourage one another, be men of light and comrades of courage to fight the good fight of faith together, in community.

You have been called to be set apart from the world. Live out your call boldly, for your life is a testimony of Jesus Christ. Through you and your marriage, others will find hope and salvation as you point them to God.

Dear Lord,

Thank You for calling me to You and calling me out. May I heed Your call to be set apart. Lord, teach me what Your Word says about me. I pray that I would adopt the things You say about me as truth in my life. Help me to walk closely in Your footsteps and help me not to stumble. I pray I will become the man that You have called me to be, not only for You, but also for myself and my bride. Help me to respond with a humble heart when another brother in Christ calls me out or if my wife calls out sin in my life. Help me be receptive. Help me to listen. Help me repent. I pray my wife and I find value in godly community.

In Jesus' name, AMEN!

Create a list of verses that describe what God is calling you to be as a husband and as a man and then pray over them asking God to make them a reality in your life. Start with the three verses listed above.

STATUS UPDATE: @husbandrevolution I have been called out by God to be a man who leads his family toward righteousness. #HusbandAfterGod

QUESTIONS:

Why is it important to know the ten commandments?

In what ways do you provide for your family?

What challenges do you experience when others or your wife calls out sin in your life?

PRAYER FOR YOU

Colossians 4:2, Hebrews 5:7, Matthew 6:9-13,
2 Chronicles 7:14, John 14, John 15, Philippians 4:6

Relationships are extremely important to God. He created you with the purpose of having an intimate friendship with Him, as well as an intimate relationship with your wife. Communication is a vital component of having a strong relationship. Just like your marriage will not sustain if you do not communicate with your wife on a daily basis, you cannot have a relationship with God if you are not willing to communicate with Him. God does not want you just to believe in Him, He wants you to engage with Him, and prayer is how you do that.

Through prayer, you can thank Him, ask of Him, and share with Him all of the details of your life. There is nothing that is too big that would be impossible for Him to handle and nothing that is too small that He would want you to leave out. God wants to hear from you daily. As you spend time praying, you will draw closer to God, and He will draw closer to you.

Jesus models how to pray in Matthew 6. Meditate on

this portion of scripture and use it as a guide when learning how to pray. You have also had the opportunity throughout this devotional to pray at the end of every chapter. Each prayer serves to encourage you and guide you in how to pray for yourself, as well as how to pray for your wife!

Prayer must be a priority in your life and your marriage. Establishing an obedience of daily prayer will keep your heart aligned with God's will and it will keep your eyes focused on Him. Be sure to share with God why you are thankful for your wife. She is a gift from Him!

There is power in prayer!

As you pray for the transformation of your character, you will begin to see change, and when you inquire for understanding, you will gain wisdom. Revealing your heart to God through prayer is an essential way to experience extraordinary intimacy with God.

Nurturing great communication is vital for any thriving relationship. Be intentional about pursuing time every day to pray for yourself. Share with God about your life, about your emotions, about the condition of your heart, about needs that you have, about your appreciation, about answered prayers, about any change you are experiencing, about the change you desire to experience and about His will. You can pray out loud, or you can pray in your heart, God hears both! Also, be intentional about listening to God. He will respond to you, perhaps in different and unique ways, but He will respond.

Dear Lord,

Thank You for the gift of prayer. I value being able to come and share my heart with You. I am also blessed to be able to lift my requests to You! Prayer builds my faith in You, it draws me close to You, and it reminds me to seek after You daily. Please put passion in my heart to pray every day. Holy Spirit please help me to understand prayer better and give me the discipline to spend quality time talking to You. I pray that You continue to transform my character. May You mold me into the man and the husband You created me to be. Fill me with Your wisdom, Your patience, Your kindness and Your great love. I pray that I would mirror Your image and that others would ask me why I have joy. I pray that in that moment You would give me the courage and the words to share Your incredible love story, Your Gospel! Give me ears to hear You! I pray protection over me from the enemy. Guard my mind against temptation, help me to stand firm in faith, and defend me against this dark world. Thank You for giving me so much! All I need is You! May Your will be done in me and through me.

In Jesus' name, AMEN!

CHALLENGE:
Start a prayer journal to keep track of your prayers, and be sure to add the answers to those prayers. It is good to recognize when prayers are answered so that you see God's faithfulness. Also, take time throughout the day to pray for yourself.

STATUS UPDATE: @husbandrevolution There is power in prayer and I will use that power in my marriage and life. #HusbandAfterGod

QUESTIONS:
Why is it important for you to pray every day?

How has the guided prayers in this devotional impacted you?

In what ways can you increase quality prayer time with God?

PRAYER FOR YOUR WIFE

---

1 Thessalonians 5:16-18, James 5:13-16,
Ephesians 6:12, Romans 8:26

Praying for your wife is one of the most powerful ways you can protect her. Praying for your wife means that you are going before God, petitioning Him to move in her heart and imploring Him to guard her.

Yielding your heart to God in prayer aligns your will with His will, your desires with His desires. When you pray for your wife, you are inviting God to enact His will in your marriage.

As you spend time praying for your wife, be sure that your motives are pure and that the change you desire to see in your wife will draw her closer to God. Be intentional about praying for your wife to experience extraordinary intimacy with God and for her to learn more about God's ways. May your intentions be based on faith that your wife will mature into the woman and wife God created her to be.

Praying with your wife is one of the most significant ways you can spiritually lead her. Do not allow thoughts of selfishness or insecurity keep you from initiating prayer with your wife. She needs you to lead her in prayer. She needs to know that you have the courage to pray for her and your marriage. Praying with and for your wife builds trust in your marriage, and it builds up security in your wife's heart.

Praying for your wife and with your wife daily is critical. Prayer requires humility, so by devoting yourself to prayer, you are keeping your heart softened toward your wife and mindful of her needs. Thus, you are cultivating an atmosphere of intimacy, where selfishness and pride cannot tear down your marriage.

When you pray for your wife, begin by thanking God for her life. Then lift up any needs she may have and always implore God's protection over her.

Remember that you are a warrior in a very real battle, a battle that is not against flesh and blood, but against the forces of the enemy. Prayer is your weapon to defend the cause of Christ, His testimony, and your wife's heart.

As much as this battle wars against you, keep in mind that it is constantly attacking your wife as well, trying to weaken her and ruin your relationship with her. Stand in God's strength, fight for your marriage and use your weapon of prayer diligently. Pray for your wife's soul, insist that God blesses her, sends her encouragement every day and fills her heart with joy. Take advantage of the opportunity you have to beseech your King and Commander for the strength to fight the good fight with faithful prayer.

Dear Lord,

Thank You for my wife. Thank You for her heart, her health, and her love for me. Remind me daily and even moment by moment to lift her up in prayer to You. I pray right now that You would bless her. Use people around her, including me to affirm her. I pray that she would be encouraged to seek after You daily for her strength and comfort. May Your Holy Spirit transform her character so that she reflects You, Lord. Help her improve in the areas she is weak and continue to strengthen her each day. May she draw close to You and may Your will be evident in her life. I pray against the powers of this dark world, I pray against temptations, I pray against the schemes of the enemy that try to attack my wife. I pray for protection in Jesus' name! Reveal to her Your wisdom and Your truths. May her soul know You well. I pray that I can help her and inspire her everyday.

In Jesus' name, AMEN!

Spend time praying for your wife. Share with God why you are thankful for her, lift up any needs she may have, pray for her character to reflect Christ, and petition God to protect her.

STATUS UPDATE: @husbandrevolution I find great joy in daily lifting my wife up in prayer to the Lord. #HusbandAfterGod

QUESTIONS:

How will praying for your wife positively impact your marriage?

What are some specific things you know your wife needs prayer for?

What fears do you have, if any, about going to your wife and praying for her out loud?

PRAYER FOR YOUR MARRIAGE

Ecclesiastes 4:12, Matthew 18:20,
Romans 12:11-13, 1 Timothy 2:8

Every day you are given choices. When you make decisions, you are choosing what impact you desire to have on you and your family. Your choices reveal whether your aim is to build up or tear down.

Your marriage is one of the first things that is directly affected by your every day choices. Your marriage is a covenant established by you and your wife. Although founded on great love for one another, your marriage relationship is not impenetrable, bulletproof, nor is it immune to the influences of this world. You must remember that your marriage will always be a vulnerable target of the enemy. You must take action to protect your marriage and build it up strong, centered on God through prayer. Talk to God about your marriage and pray earnestly for God to help you build a strong foundation for your marriage. Begin today, to build the foundation of your marriage through prayer. Praying for your marriage every day will encourage your faithfulness, bring peace to your home, and it will give God the opportunity to fulfill His will in you and through you as a husband. Submit to God through prayer and He will make Himself known to both you and your wife.

Building a solid foundation of prayer in your marriage is a priority. As the husband, it is your responsibility to lead your wife in this way. Praying with your wife is one of the most intimate experiences you will ever encounter because the two of you are going before God, together. Jesus says that when two or more are gathered in His name He is there with them. Therefore, when you lead your wife in prayer, coming together in His name to pray, Christ is there!

Do not be discouraged if your wife refuses to pray with you. Do not get frustrated, angry, or upset. Understand that her personal relationship with God will be greatly influenced by your personal relationship with God. Your obedience to God should never be contingent on your wife's actions or responses. Encourage her to pray and if she refuses, find a quiet place to spend with the Lord and pray for her. Trust God with your wife's heart and have faith that one day you will be able to experience prayer with her.

Prayer requires humility, and as you practice praying with your wife, it will become more comfortable. Appoint a time every day for prayer and always invite your wife to join you. Thank God for specific things going on in your life and then lift your requests up to Him. Pray for the day and the plans you and your wife have made, pray that your hearts are sensitive toward God and toward each other, pray over struggles that tempt you, pray protection over your relationship and always pray that God would teach you how to love each other better.

Invite God to be a part of your marriage, to walk alongside you, and on difficult days ask Him to carry you. When you and your wife are having a hard day, whether due to a conflict or perhaps health issues, or any other reason, stop everything and go to God together in prayer! Devote yourselves to pray for your marriage and experience extraordinary intimacy with your Maker, together!

Being a wise builder and intentionally strengthening the foundation of your marriage will contribute to the overall quality of your life. The foundation of your marriage will also contribute to the legacy you leave well after your time on Earth is complete. Be intentional and consider the impact of your decisions. You are accountable to your actions. Choose to be a man who prays.

Dear Lord,

Thank You for designing me with the ability to build. I pray that I would build up my marriage and family, starting with prayer. Help me lead my wife by initiating prayer. Teach me how to pray. Teach me how to be faithful to praying daily. I pray You would give me a strong desire to pray every day. I pray that as my wife and I pray together our marriage would be strengthened. Please help us build up the foundation of our marriage so that our love is lasting. I pray against the enemy's attacks against our marriage. May his plans falter and amount to nothing. I pray against any attacks he may form against my wife. Guard her heart and her mind. I pray my wife is willing to pray with me and that she is blessed by us praying together. I pray my wife's relationship with You grows deeper. Reveal Yourself to her in mighty ways. Thank You for our marriage and thank You for the gift of prayer. May we honor You and glorify You in all that we do!

In Jesus' name, AMEN!

Invite your wife to pray with you over your marriage. Here are some areas of marriage that you can pray over: intimacy, restoration, trust, forgiveness, children, finances, tithe, health, family, in-laws, job, housing, hobbies. If she refuses your invitation, find a quiet place and pray by yourself. Pray for your marriage and your wife.

STATUS UPDATE: @husbandrevolution I commit to pray for my marriage daily. #HusbandAfterGod

QUESTIONS:
How does praying with your wife build a God-centered marriage?

What keeps you from asking your wife to pray with you?

What changes need to be made so that you can pray with your wife for your marriage on a daily basis?

DAY 23

UNITY IN CHRIST

John 17, Ephesians 4, Philippians 1:27, Philippians 2:2,
Romans 12:3-13, Romans 15:1-7, 1 Peter 3:8
Hebrews 10:24-25, Acts 2:42-47, 1 Thessalonians 5:14,
1 Corinthians 12:26,

Your enemy loves to encourage isolation. He is like a lion stalking the young gazelle that strays just a little too far from the herd. Isolation and darkness are a breeding ground for sin and death. A godly marriage can never thrive in isolation. Do not be deceived to think that you and your wife can be in the will of God and have a life that is completely autonomous and without accountability. Yes, you can choose to live this way, but you will be putting your marriage and walk with Christ in danger. Do not be like that young gazelle.

God created community to protect the individuals in it. When one member suffers all suffer together; when one is honored, all celebrate. You and your wife, as believers, are not separate from the rest of the body of Christ. God desires that your marriage would be an active and valuable part of His body. Not only to contribute to the welfare and strengthening of your brothers and sisters but also to be encouraged, strengthened and built up as a couple. This idea is not that you would live in communal living, but that you would have a mind and spirit that strives toward unity and like-mindedness with the church.

Your unity with your wife is a small picture of this great unity you share with the rest of the church. In the same way, you or your wife cannot decide to live separate lives from each other and think that your marriage can go on, neither can you live secluded from the body of believers. Do you know that Jesus prayed that you and the rest of the church would be one as He and God are one, perfectly one? Jesus desires that you would understand and pursue unity with other Christians the way He has unity with God.

In today's culture, it is very acceptable to live a secret and private life. Nobody allowed to judge you or tell you what to do. Nobody to look in and see what's going on in your life and marriage. This way of living is the way the world lives, not the way followers of Jesus live, not the way biblical men live.

Begin to pray and ask that God would bring other God-fearing couples into your life. Pursue relationships with other Christian husbands who have been married longer than you. Let them inspire you to good works and holiness. Build friendships with people who are not afraid to speak truth with love into your life, to call you out when you aren't loving your wife well, and to encourage you when she isn't respecting you. People who you can laugh with and who will let you vent to when needed. Marriages that will pray for you and fight for your marriage when you feel like giving up, this is what God intended community for. Stop avoiding it and start inviting it.

Dear Lord,

Thank You for creating community and for giving me and my marriage an opportunity to be a part of a body that is bigger than us. I know that You love Your church and every part in it. Lord, bring more God fearing marriages into our lives so that we can grow in community and mature as Christians. Take away any fears or reservations we may have and replace any doubts or insecurities with confidence in Your plan for our lives. Lord, I desire to lead my family in a culture that You created, a culture of fellowship and unity.

In Jesus' name, AMEN!

Join a small group at your local church and be intentional about getting to know the other married couples in it. Pray that God leads a mature Christian married couple to come into your life.

STATUS UPDATE: @husbandrevolution God desires that my marriage would be an active and valuable part of the church. #HusbandAfterGod

QUESTIONS:
Why does the enemy desire that you live a life secluded from the rest of the body of believers?

What fears or hesitation might you have in allowing other Christians closer to you and your marriage?

What benefits can you see in fellowshipping with a godly community of other marriages?

THE PARTS OF MARRIAGE

Genesis 2:24, 1 Corinthians 12:12-27, Ephesians 5:28-33

The intricately designed human body is a made up of different parts; a foot, an ear, an eye are all individual parts, working alongside other parts to fulfill their function and the overall whole of the body. Likewise, as a Christian you become a member of Christ's body, working alongside other believers to fulfill God's will. Although everyone is given a different distribution of gifts by the Holy Spirit, they work in unity and obedience to God. As a Christian, God has called you to love and respect the body of Christ. Treating one another with respect, encouraging one another with affirmation and caring for one another with the knowledge that each part is valuable, each part is worthy.

All the more, when a husband and wife enter into the covenantal relationship of marriage, they become one flesh. Just as a body takes care of it's parts, and Jesus takes care of His body, so a husband and wife are responsible for taking care of each other as they now represent one flesh, one body, one marriage.

You are accountable for your part, and your wife is

accountable for hers. Although you are individual beings with different preferences, traits, opinions, and characteristics, God designed you to be able to work together in unity. Although you and your wife are individuals, you are not independent from one another. You belong to each other.

A thriving marriage built in unity requires humbleness, selflessness and unconditional love. With these three attributes fueling your heart, you will never grow weary of working together as one with your wife, cherishing her all the days of her life.

Be aware of how your body as a whole is doing, how your marriage is doing. If one part suffers, every part suffers with it. If one part is honored, the whole body rejoices. If your wife is suffering, stand beside her, help carry her along with compassion motivating your heart. If your wife is honored, receives acclaim or perhaps a promotion, celebrate with her. Be a husband eager to fulfill your wife's needs, knowing that the result will benefit your marriage as a whole. Never stop trying, never stop loving, never give up.

Dear Lord,

Thank You for the illustration of how all believers make up one body, Your body. We are all given different purposes, we are all uniquely made and gifted, and we all have different roles, yet we are all significant. Thank You for showing me that. Lord, help me to remember every day that my wife and I are one body. Use this revelation to transform my way of looking at my marriage. We are not two individuals, but one entity working to move Your kingdom forward in the world. We are one unit meant to bring You glory and honor. Thank You for this gift that is my marriage.

In Jesus' name, AMEN!

Find one way to bless the body of Christ, whether it is encouraging someone or fulfilling a need. Also, do one thing to bless your body, your marriage.

STATUS UPDATE: @husbandrevolution I will love my wife as my own body, cherishing her heart and nourishing her soul as Christ does the church. #HusbandAfterGod

QUESTIONS:
What does the Bible mean that you and your wife become one?

How does 1 Corinthians 12:26 play out in your marriage? Share examples.

Just like you take care of your body daily, what are some things you can do to take care of your marriage daily to maintain it and keep it healthy?

GOD'S ORDER

Exodus 20:3, 1 Corinthians 14:33, 1 Corinthians 11:3,
Ephesians 5:23, Romans 13:1-2, 1 Corinthians 7:4,
Genesis 1:28, Matthew 28:18, John 19:10-11, 1 Timothy 2,
Matthew 20:28, Mark 10:7-9, Mark 10:41-45

Our God is a god of order. He outlines in His Word the order to which you should operate as a man of faith. The more you spend time reading the Bible, the more understanding you will gain in regards to God's divine order. With the Holy Spirit leading you, your life will produce godliness, and you will desire to operate in the order and authority given by God.

All authority is derived from God.

Authority does not come from within yourself. You cannot bestow upon yourself authority. Authority is given and entrusted to you by God through Christ. Your wife's head of authority is you, your head of authority is Christ and Christ's head of authority is God. This is written out in scripture according to God's order.

It is critical that you take the authority given to you seriously, acknowledging who your authority is, and where your authority comes from. Being a man of divine order and leading your family in God's ways, requires authority. However, you must never use the authority you have to mistreat or abuse anyone. Your authority is not a tool to bend others to your will. Your authority was not granted to you so that you can be a controlling, manipulative husband and father. Your authority is power given to you to fulfill the will of God and you are held accountable to your head, who is Christ.

Remember to gain an understanding of how to best use your authority by studying your model and head, Jesus Christ. God's Word says that Jesus did not come to be served, rather He came to serve. You must never lord your authority over others or exercise authority outside of God's will for selfish gain. With the authority you have been given, serve others in love. Draw them closer to the Heavenly Father, just as Jesus does.

God desires that you appropriately operate out of the authority given to you from above to fulfill your role as the head of your home. You are responsible to your wife and children; to model for them godliness and to teach them God's ways.

In God's order, He says that you are the head of your wife. Your relationship with your wife is the second most important priority in your life. Lead her with confidence. Cherish her and love her. If Christ is your head and you choose not to submit to Him, you can't possibly expect your wife to submit to you. Yet, if you do submit to Christ and you exercise your authority to fulfill all that God has commanded you, it will be extremely difficult for your wife to not want to submit to you.

Being a man of faith, a warrior, a protector, a brave and mighty man of valor, being a man of godliness requires a heart after God. When you submit to God's order and God's authority, your life will be transformed. You will have a great understanding of your purpose and the role you have been given in this life. Order your life according to the Word of God and establish order in everything you do. By being a faithful man of order you reflect God's character, you are an ambassador of Christ's testimony, you provide security and trust within your family, and a respectable reputation among many.

Dear Lord,

Thank You for Your divine order. I have so much security knowing that You are not a God of confusion or chaos. Thank You for entrusting me with authority to lead my wife and family. I understand the seriousness of the authority You have given to me so that I may fulfill Your purpose for me as the head of my home. I pray I never exercise the authority given to me for personal gain or selfish reasons. I pray I use this authority with self-control to protect and provide for my family, while teaching them Your ways. I pray I can serve them in humbleness. I pray I can provide security and trust for my family. May Your Holy Spirit help me learn to be appropriate and righteous as I yield my heart to You in submission. I pray that I am a man of order who reflects Your order through my behavior and through the fruitfulness in my life. I pray I can love my wife unconditionally just as Christ loves His bride. May You be glorified forever and ever.

In Jesus name amen!

Meditate on the enormity of this revelation. Your authority is derived from Christ. He is the one you will stand before and give an account for how you lead your wife and kids.

STATUS UPDATE: @husbandrevolution Order your marriage and life according to the Word of God. #HusbandAfterGod

JOURNAL QUESTIONS:

How does having order help provide security in a family?

What examples, of how to best love your wife, did Jesus model for you?

In what ways do you struggle with using your authority for selfish gain?

AVOIDING GOD

Genesis 3:8, Jeremiah 17:10, Jeremiah 23:24,
1 Chronicles 28:9, Hebrews 12:1-6, James 4:17,
Proverbs 28:13, 1 John 1:8-10, Galatians 5:19-21,
2 Timothy 2:22, Luke 8:17, Romans 6:23, Romans 12:1-2,
Proverbs 18:1

When the first man sinned against God, he hid. Adam knew what he had done was wrong. Shame and guilt flooded his heart and mind. Unity and intimacy with God was severed. Adam hid because he didn't want God to know what he had done and he didn't want to confront the consequences of his actions. Adam avoided God.

Have you been hiding from God? Do you avoid Him because of shame from sin? Are there areas of your life you are keeping a secret from Him?

Sin will ruin your relationship with God. Sin destroys intimacy and keeps you burdened by fear, shame and guilt. Sin will convince you that you are unworthy to pray or unworthy to be in the presence of other believers. Sin will make you feel uncomfortable in the presence of holiness. Sin will convince you to isolate yourself from God, from your wife, and from your community. Sin is darkness. The consequence of sin is death.

Without a repentant heart, sin will consume and destroy you and your marriage.

Sin begins as a thought and then moves into the heart as an intention that gets carried out through actions.

When the first man sinned against God, he hid with his wife. Together they hid from God. Adam was not alone when he sinned. Although he independently chose to sin, his wife was an influence in his life. Then together they hid from God. A husband and wife have a strong ability to influence each other. Even with that ability they can choose to influence toward godliness or they can influence toward ungodliness. The influence pours out from their actions, behaviors and words.

You have the ability to influence your wife. Your behavior will dictate the way in which you are influencing her. As the head of your wife, you are held accountable for how you influence your wife. A wise husband will influence his wife to turn her heart toward God, not away.

A faithful man will confront his sin, repent of his wrongdoing, and reconcile his heart to God. A righteous man will resist the temptation to sin with every fiber of his being. As a man after God, a man who desires to worship and please God, a man who is himself a living sacrifice holy and acceptable, a man who has an intimate relationship with God, you will experience the extraordinary miracle of transformation and sanctification. You will experience the victory that exists only in Christ. Victory over strongholds and sin. Victory in your marriage. Victory with your children.

Victory upon victory upon victory. You are not a victim of your sin. Sin does not just happen to you without your consent. Do not believe this lie that you are still a slave to sin. No, you have been set free from sin and have become a slave of righteousness.

Even Though Adam hid from God; God found him. Even if you try to hide, God will find you. Everything that is in the darkness will be exposed by the light.

Dear Lord,

I pray that I would not hide from You. I pray Your light would fill my entire life and that any amount of darkness would flee far from me. Lord, help me open my heart to You so that You may get to know me. I repent of the sin in my life, and I ask You to set me free from any bondage. I pray that as I influence my wife, it would only be toward righteousness. I pray I can be a good example for my wife, a person she can trust and admire. May my character be a reflection of Your Holy character. I pray that my life reflects Your testimony and that my marriage is a powerful message of Your ability to heal and restore. Help me not to be oppressed by feelings of shame, defeat, unrest, fear or guilt. I pray for freedom! I pray truthfulness fills my heart. I pray I never lie and never hide from You or my wife again. Thank You for Your amazing light and thank You for Your grace. I pray I am a man of faithfulness.

In Jesus name amen!

CHALLENGE:

Is there anything you need to confess? Drag your sin into the light by confessing and repenting of it to God and your wife. Yes, this will be uncomfortable, maybe even painful, but it will be worth it.

STATUS UPDATE: @husbandrevolution I have been set free from sin and have become a slave of righteousness. #HusbandAfterGod

JOURNAL QUESTIONS:

What are some reasons you hide from God or hide from your wife?

Why does hiding seem easier than telling the truth?

In what ways have you influenced your wife toward righteousness or sin?

ABIDING IN GOD

John 15, James 4:7, 2 John 1:9, Galatians 2:20,
John 10:28-29, John 8:31, John 1:1, Galatians 5:22-23,
Psalm 34:8, Hebrews 12:6, James 4:8

The flash of car lights caught the attention of a mother and father who were chatting with another couple out front of their home. Their young son had been playing by their side. However, the moment the lights turned the street corner, panic flared up in their hearts. The father immediately called out to his son, "Stop!" The boy's toes curled over the edge of the curb, his body bracing in self-control, his head slightly turned over his shoulder to acknowledge his father.

The dad commanded his son to come to him, and the boy obeyed immediately. "Son, good job stopping when daddy called out to you. Good job listening to my voice. I asked you to stop because you were headed toward the street and that is dangerous because cars drive in the street. You must never play in the street. Okay?" The father hugged his son tightly and whispered in his ear, "I love you." The father's heart pounded from the fear of his son being harmed by the passing car. Relief came quickly. The son continued playing safely, now in closer proximity to his parents.

The son loved and obeyed his father because his father first loved him. The father's love built a foundation of trust and respect in their relationship. The training and discipline to teach the child to listen to the father's voice and obey immediately was worth the energy and effort exerted. It saved the child's life.

You are a child of God, and He is your Heavenly Father. As you abide in God, you will be trained and disciplined by the Father, a process of transformation that grows your character. To abide means to accept God's ways without objection, to be faithful and submissive to Him and to remain in intimate communion with Him. To abide in God means that you spend quality time studying His Word, for the Word is God. To abide in God means that you remain faithful and steadfast, no matter what circumstances you face in this life. God is your refuge and your strength. When you abide in God you yield your heart to Him, you give your life to Him, you trust Him, and you obey Him, a response of love for the love He has poured out for you.

Obedience is the proof that you are abiding. Obedience is the way you live your life in agreement with God's will. Obedience is choosing to live God's ways. More proof is the evidence of your character producing fruitfulness.

You, your wife and your children will all benefit from your fruitfulness. As a husband after God, your fruitfulness will provide an atmosphere of peace and holiness in your home. As a man who abides in God, faithful to lead his family spiritually, your fruitfulness will allow your family to taste the goodness of the Lord.

Abiding in God is where the training happens to be a valiant warrior, a loving husband, and a great father. Abiding in God is where you will experience close companionship with God, and you will experience intimacy with God. You will get to know Him deeper as you seek after Him.

Choose to be a man who aims to produce fruitfulness in your life. Care about your character and the impact it has on others. Choose to be a man who abides in God. Choose to be a son who hears the Father's voice. The choice is yours, and the choice is present every single day as you consider how you spend your time. Choose to abide and witness how God transforms your life.

Dear Lord,

Please help me to remain in You. I pray my heart is sensitive to Your Word. I pray my ears are sensitive to Your voice, that I may hear You when You speak to me. I pray for wisdom and courage to do all that You ask of me. Holy Spirit, I pray You would convict my heart when I sin and lead me to repentance. I pray that I would be obedient to Your Word and that my life would produce fruitfulness. I pray that as I abide in You, my wife will also have a growing desire to abide in You. I pray that I would gain wisdom and that I would understand Your Holy Word. Help me to memorize Your Word and give me a passionate desire to know it well. I pray You would help me teach Your Word to my wife and family. Transform us, Lord! Transform our marriage!

In Jesus name amen!

CHALLENGE:

Consider three ways you can obey God and abide in Him this week and make these three ways your goals for the week.

STATUS UPDATE: @husbandrevolution I choose to be a man who aims to produce fruitfulness in my life and marriage through abiding in Christ. #HusbandAfterGod

JOURNAL QUESTIONS:

What does it look like to abide in God on a daily basis?

How does reading God's Word help produce good fruit in your life?

What benefits does your family gain from you abiding in God?

INTIMACY IN MARRIAGE

Colossians 3:19, Genesis 2:24, 1 Corinthians 7:3-5,
1 John 4:7-8

You are an intimate being, designed to experience and maintain deeply intimate relationships. You were made with the ability to listen, to communicate, to comfort, and to feel a wide range of emotions. You were made for relationships.

God pursues you with an invitation to join Him in a love relationship, and He desires that you get to experience the richness of intimacy with your wife. Your marriage is a symbol and representation of the intimate relationship between Jesus and His bride, the church, a correlation and mystery that is incredibly profound. Knowing this mystery will help you understand how you are supposed to love your wife. Meditate on it, consider its depth, pray for understanding to rule in your heart.

Intimacy is the most important part of your marriage. Intimacy with your wife is much more than sex. Although sex is a vital part of intimacy, it is not everything. Intimacy is where you and your wife grow to know each other more than you will ever know anyone else. Together you experience what it means to be one. Intimacy is becoming familiar with one another, which only happens when you spend quality time with each other.

There are three essential ways of experiencing intimacy in marriage, all of which are vital for a healthy and thriving marriage. Physical intimacy, engaging in physical affection such as hand holding, kissing, and sex is important for both the husband and wife to feel wanted and loved by each other. Emotional intimacy, such as having a deep conversation with one another and validating feelings, is a key component to fulfilling each other's need for security and connectedness. The last main facet that is critical to the overall health of your marriage is spiritual intimacy, including reading scripture and praying together.

Initiating intimacy in your relationships will be challenging at times, but remember you were made for this. Just do it! God's purpose for your marriage is for you, and your wife, to experience a love relationship, passionately pursuing each other daily, where the ups and downs of life draw you closer together and closer to Him, a place where true intimacy thrives.

Similar to your relationship with God, cultivating intimacy in marriage requires vulnerability. The more effort you and your wife intentionally put forth to reveal yourselves deeply to each other, the more familiar you two will become. In so doing, your marriage will be blessed, and your marital foundation will be fortified.

Intimacy in marriage is part of God's great design. Genesis 2 recognizes that a husband and wife become one flesh. This concept of oneness was deliberate and significant, encouraging a husband and wife to humble themselves for the sake of the other and to seek the benefit of the whole of them as one flesh. As you and your wife live as one flesh, intimacy is experienced, and love is cultivated.

There are many ways to increase intimacy in marriage and nurture oneness, including some of the following:

- Having honest and transparent conversations about faith, life and marriage.
- Initiating sexual intimacy
- Confessing sins
- Praying together
- Going on date nights
- Pursuing each other passionately
- Talking about goals and dreams
- Serving each other
- Blessing each other

Building a healthy, joyful, God-centered marriage where intimacy thrives is the only option for a godly man, but it takes time and energy to attain it. It builds up over time as trust, confidence and faithfulness are produced. You are responsible for fulfilling your part and your wife is responsible for hers. Your marriage will reach this fulfillment when both of you are working together towards oneness. However, God calls you to remain steadfast in doing your part regardless of whether your wife is doing hers or not. Let love motivate you and fuel your heart to persevere. Your marriage is worth it; it will always be worth it.

Dear Lord,

Thank You for the complexity of Your Word. Thank You for the complexity of Your design. To know that You built me for relationships is awesome and I desire to embrace a truly intimate relationship with You and with my wife. Lord, You have created us with so much depth. I pray that as a husband, I would learn to understand the complexities of intimacy with my wife. God, I know that sex is not the only way to be intimate. Help me to be intimate with my wife not only physically, but also emotionally, mentally and spiritually. I pray that I would pursue my wife physically by letting her know that I am attracted to her and that I love her deeply. Help me to make our marriage a safe place emotionally so that she will feel free to invite me into her heart and trust me with her feelings. Lord, help me to live with my wife in understanding so that I can stimulate her mentally and show her that I want to know the way she thinks. Lastly Lord, teach me to lead us deeper into a more intimate relationship with You. Help me to pray with her for everything and in everything. I pray that I would read to her and with her and that I would remind her of what Your Word says over specific areas of our lives. Lord, let me be intimate with my wife on every level.

In Jesus name amen!

Invite your wife to have an intimate conversation to discuss how you can grow to know each other more. Start by sharing with her something that she doesn't know about you. Never neglect the pursuit of knowing your wife deeper.

STATUS UPDATE: @husbandrevolution Building a healthy, joyful, God-centered marriage where intimacy thrives is the only option for a godly man.#HusbandAfterGod

JOURNAL QUESTIONS:
In what ways can you be more intimate with your wife?

Why is it important for you to pursue a loving relationship with your wife every day?

Why is listening and talking such an essential part of being intimate?

WALK IN VICTORY

Galatians 5:16-26, 1 John 3:6, Deuteronomy 20:4,
Romans 6:6, Romans 6:11-18, 1 Corinthians 15:57,
Romans 8:31-39, 1 Corinthians 10:13, John 16:33,
Matthew 5:19

Every day you are given choices. Some choices you make are small and seemingly insignificant while others are clearly crucial with an impact to be life changing. The truth is that every choice you have to make is valuable and significant. Every choice you are given should be considered with a heart that is yielded to God. Every step you take has a ripple effect.

As you consider your steps, you must acknowledge the truth that you have the ability to walk in victory because of the victory of Christ. As you abide in the Lord, you are granted freedom from sin, no longer condemned, no longer a slave to sin.

Although you have victory in Christ, this does not mean that you will never experience temptation, even our Lord and Savior was subject to temptation. But with each temptation that comes your way you have a choice; a choice to give in or a choice to walk in the victory that

Christ has already given you. God is your strength, and He will always provide a way out of temptation, but it is your responsibility to resist sin and be above reproach.

If you are in Christ, then you must not live in habitual sin. When you are saved by God's grace, and you are abiding in God, your life changes.

Of course, the enemy does not like that you believe and trust in God. He will attempt to attack you and your family. He will tempt you and urge you to break unity with God and your wife. He will try to oppress you so that you give up. You will be challenged to believe the lies that try to keep you entangled in sin. You will be tempted to justify your sin.

You must stay strong and you must persevere in righteousness. You must dispel the lies that lure you to believe that your struggle with sin is a part of who you are, that you will always struggle with it or that you can overcome it on your own. Take the example from Jesus, who when tempted conquered the temptation by knowing and proclaiming scripture.

Walk in victory! Death and sin have been defeated through Jesus Christ. You have victory through Him, and you have freedom from sin!

You are no longer a slave to sin; rather you are a slave to righteousness. You must speak this over your life daily, reminding yourself that you have victory in Christ.

Sin doesn't just happen to you. Sin is always a choice, so choose righteousness today!

Dear Lord,

Thank You for the complete redeeming work of Your Son, Jesus Christ. Without His sacrifice and resurrection, I would still be dead in my sin and a slave to temptations. Lord, because of You I have been set free from the bonds of sin and can now walk in complete freedom. I pray that I would walk in this victory every day. I know that even though I am no longer a slave to sin I still have the ability to choose to sin, and I acknowledge that sin is not something that just happens to me. Holy Spirit, remind me to say no to sin and yes to righteousness. I pray that I would present my body to You daily to be used as an instrument of righteousness. I pray that I would be fully convinced that I am more than a conqueror through Your power living in me. Thank You Lord, for the gift of freedom. I pray that I never take it for granted.

In Jesus name amen!

Find some scripture that you can memorize and use to combat temptations when they come. For Example, read Romans 6:6.

STATUS UPDATE: @husbandrevolution Walk in victory! Death and sin have been defeated through Jesus Christ. #HusbandAfterGod

JOURNAL QUESTIONS:
What hinders you from believing you can walk in true victory, free from sin?

What sin, if any, have you had the most difficulty having victory over?

How can you be strengthened to resist the temptations to sin?

THE HUSBAND REVOLUTION

Matthew 26:36-44

He sat in church with his head in his hands, frustrated and overwhelmed about the state of his marriage. He desired to be fulfilled, but it seemed like nothing was going to fix the issues between him and his wife.

While the man struggled in despair, God pressed it upon his heart to remember the story of Jesus praying in the garden. Just hours before He would be nailed to the cross, Jesus Himself wrestled with the circumstances at hand.

Three times Jesus cried out to God, "May this cup pass from me..." and three times He followed up with this prayer, "May your will be done." Jesus surrendered Himself to the will of God, motivated by unconditional love for His bride and obedience to His Father in heaven.

The man, struggling to understand his marriage circumstance, saw the ultimate picture of marriage displayed through Christ. Regardless of whether people would receive Jesus's sacrifice and believe in Him, He went to the cross anyways. His love was unconditional, and His love made it possible to experience intimacy with God.

The man's heart began to change and soften. He realized his purpose as a husband was to love his wife like Christ, unconditionally. Regardless of whether his wife would ever receive his love, regardless of whether their marital issues were fixed, regardless of whether or not their marriage would meet all of his expectations, he was called to love his wife through it all.

The husband went to his wife and apologized to her for not loving and cherishing her as he should have been doing all along. He explained how unmet expectations crippled him and left him frustrated and bitter. He shared with her the revelation he had about Christ praying in the garden, how He surrendered Himself through the power of unconditional love to carry out God's will and how this was a representation of marriage.

Lifting his hands up to hold his wife's face, he gently embraced her and then he promised to love her like Christ for as long as they both should live.

The Husband Revolution started in the heart of Christ. The revolution is a movement to live differently than the world and embrace God's divine will. The husband revolution for every man starts with accepting the truth of this revelation about Christ in the garden.

Being a husband after God requires you to abide in God so that your character is transformed to be like His. The Husband Revolution is a passionate commitment to cherish your wife and to love her unconditionally. It requires you to lead her by serving her, just as Jesus came to serve.

The Husband Revolution is a call for all men to rise and be men of the Word, men who are faithful to God and faithful to their wives, men who fight the good fight with bravery and wisdom. Thus, changing the world for the better, a true victory that only comes through Christ.

You are a man, created in the image of God. You have been equipped to walk in righteousness. You have purpose and you have immeasurable influence in the spiritual growth of your wife and children.

Rise and join the revolution!

Be blessed, be affirmed and be honored as you pursue your role as a husband after God.

Dear Lord,

Thank You for sending Your Son to the cross for my salvation and freedom. Thank You for showing me grace and mercy. Lord, You are worthy of all praise, and I desire to know You more. I pray that I would begin a revolution in my marriage. I pray that my heart would be revived and rejuvenated. I will walk in integrity and uprightness. I will stand for my wife. I will fight against my true enemy and not against my bride. I will run to You when I am weak. I will flee temptation when it comes. I will forgive. I will repent. I will keep you at the center of my marriage. Change my mind and heart and make me more like You. Teach me to love like You, to serve like You and to walk like You. My marriage will no longer be the same because I surrender to Your will.

In Jesus' name amen!

Go to your wife and tell her that you commit to love her unconditionally and that you will lead your family by the grace and the Word of God. Tell her that you desire to love her as Christ loves His church.

STATUS UPDATE: @husbandrevolution The Husband Revolution is a call for men to rise & be men of the Word, who are faithful & love like Christ. #HusbandAfterGod

JOURNAL QUESTIONS:
Why is the revelation of Jesus in the garden a powerful message to understand?

How does abiding in God help you love your wife?

What steps will it take for you to lead your wife and family according to God's ways?

If this devotional has impacted your faith and marriage please let me know by posting a testimony here: HusbandAfterGod.com

For more marriage resources please visit:
husbandrevolution.com/marriage-resources/

Receive daily prayer for your marriage via email:
husbandrevolution.com/daily-prayer/

Get connected:
Facebook.com/husbandrevolution
Instagram.com/husbandrevolution
Twitter.com/husbandrevo

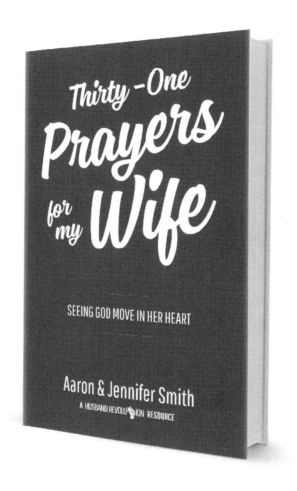

Shop.HusbandRevolution.com

I LOVE MY WIFE SHIRTS AND HOODIES AVAILABLE AT HTTP://SHOP.HUSBANDREVOLUTION.COM